KU-451-229

# Jo Brand

## Can't Stand Up For Sitting Down

headline
review

Copyright © 2010 Jo Brand

The right of Jo Brand to be identified as the Author of
the Work has been asserted by her in accordance with the
Copyright, Designs and Patents Act 1988.

First published in 2010 by HEADLINE REVIEW
An imprint of HEADLINE BOOK PUBLISHING

First published in paperback in 2011 by HEADLINE REVIEW

1

Apart from any use permitted under UK copyright law, this publication may
only be reproduced, stored, or transmitted, in any form, or by any means,
with prior permission in writing of the publishers or, in the case of
reprographic production, in accordance with the terms
of licences issued by the Copyright Licensing Agency.

Every effort has been made to fulfil requirements with regard to reproducing
copyright material. The author and the publisher will gladly rectify any
omissions at the earliest opportunity.

Cataloguing in Publication Data is available from the British Library

ISBN 978 0 7553 5528 0

Typeset in Caslon540 BT by Palimpsest Book Production Limited,
Falkirk, Stirlingshire

Printed and bound in Great Britain by
Clays Ltd, St Ives plc

Headline's policy is to use papers that are natural, renewable and
recyclable products and made from wood grown in sustainable forests.
The logging and manufacturing processes are expected to conform to the
environmental regulations of the country of origin.

HEADLINE PUBLISHING GROUP
An Hachette UK Company
338 Euston Road
London NW1 3BH

www.headline.co.uk
www.hachette.co.uk

To my family, for shoring me up during the process

| London Borough of Lambeth | |
| --- | --- |
| LM 1208376   3 | |
| **Askews & Holts** | 20-May-2011 |
| 920 BRA | £7.99 |
| | |

# Acknowledgements

I'd like to thank my family for being a great big lovely bolster separating me from the more chilly parts of the outside world, and for putting up with me while I was trying to write this as I was a right grump. I'd also like to thank my friend and agent Vivienne for being supportive, honest, and reading each bit that I sent her straight away, rather than pretending her email wasn't working. And of course I'm contractually obliged to thank Martin my editor . . . I'm sure we'll be speaking again soon. Thanks too to Alan Davies and Mark Kelly who filled in the gaps of my fading memory. And finally, I'd like to thank you for buying it – or running the risk of nicking it, if that is what you did – and I truly hope it's a good read with some laughs.

# Contents

BEING JO BRAND

# Author's Note

Hello, readers – and welcome to Part 2 of my memoirs, covering the period from my first gig as a professional comic through to the present day.

I've called them 'memoirs' because, rather than being a chronological account of my life, they're a collection of the bits and pieces of my existence that I can remember – and believe you me, I'm stunned I have recalled so much, given that my memory has been shot to pieces since I had children, and it wasn't that great before either.

I imagine that, at some point, some scientist or other has said that we only remember the exciting bits in our lives, and let's hope that's true, because you certainly don't want to know about the great cup of tea I had in April 1994 in a café in Wisbech or my favourite episode of *Casualty*.

So I hope this hotchpotch of musings is to your taste, and I can assure you they are certainly not as intellectually challenging as Proust (in case you are a bit weird and actually thought they might be). And if you start reading and think, *God, this is dull*, you can always pass it on to someone you don't like.

# TRYING TO BE FUNNY

# Shaky Beginnings

It's April 1988, and I am on Channel Four live on *Friday Night Live*. I'm on a raised platform in front of a crowd of the thinnest, youngest, most attractive people I've ever seen who are staring quizzically at me. This may well be because TV directors of live shows tend to put the chubby, not so attractive ones at the back. A part of me feels slightly smug that for once I am not at the back . . . I'm in the front, so bollocks to them.

My first couple of lines work well and there is some laughter and the crowd starts to relax a bit. I'm beginning to relax too despite the fact that my arm is going up and down in a chicken-flapping-its-wings style with nervousness. I drone on in my monotone voice . . .

Then a voice cuts through the crowd. 'Get off!'

My first feeling is one of indignation. I'm actually doing all right, so what's that all about?

Because it's live TV, the fear is multiplied a hundredfold. Any mistake you make, a small fluff or whether you spectacularly and waterfall-like actually wet yourself, will be captured for eternity – and so the pressure on you is huge. There will not be the comforting thought of a film editor whooshing away your moment of humiliation. This is it.

What do I do? It is a male voice heckling me, surprise surprise, and it is my natural inclination to get into a slanging match with him. After all, this is what we comics are supposed to do best. However, this is live telly and my set is timed to the second. If I start getting stuck into a heckler, that will eat up my time and the whole thing will be thrown out of kilter. I stare in the general direction of the heckler and say, 'Thank you,' and move on. Afterwards, however, I'm really pissed off and want to get the heckler into a corner and lamp him. My first-ever appearance on TV and he nearly ruined the whole thing.

I hear through the grapevine that some staff from LWT have been sacked that day and he is among the disgruntled sackees. I feel slightly less homicidal towards him. I suppose at least it wasn't that personal.

In a strange karmic twist, some years later I meet the heckler at a TV studio in Southampton. He is now the presenter of a live magazine show on which I am appearing.

'I was the one who heckled you on *Friday Night Live*,' he says, with a smug grin on his face.

'And now you're presenting a live show, how would *you* like to be heckled?' I enquire.

And I rather meanly leave it at that, implying that I am going to heckle him back, but not bothering, hoping the anticipatory fear will be enough to ruin his day.

Having taken the plunge in early 1988 and left my job as Senior Sister at the Maudsley Hospital – my little safety net, though I suppose most people wouldn't see a twenty-four-hour Psychiatric Emergency Clinic quite in this way – I am suddenly out on my own.

Obviously it's a bit of a risk, to leave a secure job which I liked and strike out into the murky waters of possible nothingness. Although a nurse's salary wasn't much to write home about, at least it was regular and there was always the possibility that my burgeoning comedy career could take a nose-dive before it had even begun. I had been a nurse for the last ten years, six of those years fulltime in the Emergency Clinic dealing with every possible psychiatric crisis you could imagine, from extreme psychosis to drug withdrawal to personality disorders. I had a mortgage to pay on a flat and plenty of outgoings.

Comedy, by contrast, was a hand-to-mouth existence in which, at the end of every show, you got a little brown envelope with cash in it or just a handful of notes. I wasn't sure there would be enough bookings to justify my leaving a secure job, so I asked my mum and dad what they thought about it, and they were pretty positive. They could see I'd done my time in a stable job, and to some extent were there as a safety net. They weren't loaded, but they would ensure that I wasn't on the street in a sleeping bag eating out of skips round the back of Sainsbury's.

Friends were also very supportive and thought it was hugely exciting. One particular mate had encouraged me right at the beginning by reminding me that I was never going to do it if I didn't take the plunge, and this next stage, of sloughing off my job, was something most of my friends urged me to do.

Added to that, I was bloody knackered and I really

wanted some lie-ins. Given that most of the jobs I had done up until that point had involved shift work, I fancied a bit of staying in bed till midday with nothing to do until the evening. Comedy also seemed to me to have a built-in social life, and comics seemed like interesting people. I was aware of the dearth of women and wanted to get out there and do some material for the female audience. It wasn't a particularly difficult decision. I've always been somewhat of a gambler because I don't think those huge decisions are irreversible: you can always go back. So while many people are lying awake at night turning a problem over and over in their mind, I am one of the lucky ones who snores their head off, happily oblivious of life's possible pitfalls.

Back to *Friday Night Live*, the comedy extravaganza on Channel Four which is the show for all ambitious alternative comedians to aim for at the time. The compere is Ben Elton, the politically motivated, sparkily relentless nemesis of Margaret Thatcher – every right-thinking alternative comic's sworn enemy.

The show is a hotchpotch of stand-up comedy, sketches and music. I'd found my way onto it because I was invited to attend an audition at the Brixton rehearsal rooms to prove to some people behind a desk that I was worthy of four and a half minutes of jokes on live telly.

There's nothing more demoralising for a comic than an unpissed, unsmiling panel of judges in broad daylight staring at you as you struggle through your routine doing your best to keep it upbeat. It has to be said, though, that in my case my delivery was about as upbeat as a funeral sermon, given that I had slipped into an approximation of the way the football scores are read out through a combination of nerves and ignorance. I was finding it impossible to sound like anything other than a depressed bloke with an inability to manage verbal light and shade. However, despite this they booked me and the experience was exciting and terrifying in equal measure.

Of course, having never done telly before I was swept along in a miasma of glamour and fear, doing a sound check, sitting in my dressing room telling myself all the clichés such as, 'You've made it' and stuff like that whilst glaring at my overlit face in a light-bulbed mirror. I was sandwiched between the Pogues and Mark Thomas, dressing-room-wise. A strange place to be. I reckon the Pogues had had a half or twelve, as at one point what sounded like a bar-room brawl erupted in their dressing room involving shouting and the sound of wood splintering. I would have been disappointed if they hadn't, though.

On the other side, with my door slightly open to catch the maximum effect of my virgin telly appearance, I could hear Mark Thomas negotiating with the producers about the level of bad language he was permitted to use. I'm sure I heard the sentence, 'If you get rid of a "wanker" you can have two "toffee bollocks".' Aah, the poetry of comedy.

Mark Thomas was always an electrifying presence on the comedy circuit. I remember seeing him very early on at the Comedy Store before I dipped my toe into what can be the terrifying cauldron of death on a Friday night. He seemed so big, self-confident and he filled the stage. I think the audience was probably a bit scared of him, and I recall thinking to myself that perhaps his approach was the way forward, like a no-nonsense teacher – don't give 'em a chance.

After my appearance on *Friday Night Live* which everyone seemed to agree had gone OK, I sat back and waited for the offers to flood in. Quite what sort of offers I expected I'm not sure, but whatever they were in my head, they didn't flood, they didn't even trickle.

Jo Brand

So it was back to the circuit for a bit, to practise my act around the London comedy scene.

One great thing did come out of *Friday Night Live* and that was that I got myself an agent. Naively, I didn't even realise it was something I should do, and my idea of an agent was a short balding American bloke with a very loud voice and a big cigar, going on endlessly about percentages and auditions.

Vivienne Clore approached me after the programme and asked if she could take me on . . . as it were. I can't remember much about our initial conversation and my powers of judgement were not up to much as I had no idea what I was looking for. But Vivienne seemed articulate, intelligent, cynical, a bit scary and good fun. And at the time that was good enough for me.

Vivienne is still my agent so I obviously made a good choice . . . for me. Agents seem to come in all shapes and sizes. Some are like over-attentive parents, constantly on hand to sort out the smallest problem in your life; others are like your mates, who go out on the town with you, get pissed, take drugs and sleep with you, while others are like the head of a Mafia family. You can take your pick. Vivienne and I have become good friends, but are not in each other's pockets, which I think is important. I can't envisage ever being unfaithful to her.

Vivienne has always been incredibly professional and comes from a big 'talent' agency, The Richard Stone Partnership. She's been very supportive towards me and has religiously turned up at every single Tom, Dick and Harry of a programme, however potentially rubbish it's been. But the other thing I appreciate is her honesty.

It's very hard when you work in telly and get to a certain stage in your career to get an honest answer. Now I realise I haven't got to the Madonna part of my career (and never will) where I do exactly what I like and no one can give me any advice about the direction in which I am going. On the whole, if people think that something you have done is complete rubbish, their preferred approach is to pretend that it (and you) don't really exist, rather than telling you the truth. This makes it very hard to get an objective opinion.

Of course, Vivienne doesn't go in for personality-destroying invective. If something hasn't gone well or has been definitely dodgy, she will acknowledge that and suggest changes. Similarly, my husband will tell me if something wasn't so good. Basically, however famous you are, if you retain any vestiges of true perspective, you will know yourself when you've been shite.

In those days, there was a certain hierarchy of clubs – the little sweet ones in the back room of a pub and the bigger, higher earners like the Comedy Store and Jongleurs, which had more of a ring of glamour about them and meant you didn't have to change or put your lipstick on in a toilet, kitchen or corridor.

# The Circuit,
# Not Always Electric

When I came onto the comedy circuit in 1986, it had been going for a few years already.

My friend Mark Kelly, with whom I write, remembers that when he started in 1984, there were only a handful of venues. Added to that, in the early days, the circuit seemed to have room for acts that were not just pure stand-ups. You could see a number of poets and also other people who were more like performance artists than stand-ups.

My top six acts, for their weirdness, were:

*1. Tony Green and Ian Hinchcliffe*
These two heckled me off at my first-ever gig. Tony Green did a character called Mad Jock Macock, which I feel is self-explanatory, while Ian Hinchcliffe would do things like eating glass, stripping naked and rolling on the floor on broken glass. Didn't float my boat, but we all have different tastes.

*2. Kevin McAleer*
Kevin was an absurdist whose act at the time consisted of a slideshow – although the only slide I can remember was one of a baby owl with huge eyes. Audiences seemed mesmerised by Kevin's strangeness and he sat among the stand-ups like your bonkers uncle at a family party.

*3. The Ice Man*
The Ice Man truly was a performance artist. He would try to melt a huge block of ice in a variety of ways including fire and salt, whilst a tape of opera and sounds of the sea played over it. He had two other acts: one in which he would build a crane, and another which consisted solely of him dragging a huge anchor chain across the stage. Can't see that on *Britain's Got Talent* . . . or can I?

## 4. *Arloe Barloe*

This man did an act with huge extendable arms. I can say no more than this.

## 5. *Fanny Farts*

Never has the phrase 'It does what it says on the tin' been more apt. This woman, FF, was a regular for a while at the Tunnel Club in Greenwich, and she blew raspberries out of her vagina. The capricious audience at the Tunnel would love her or hate her, depending on what mood they were in. It wasn't pornographic in the sense that she felt compelled to display said vagina, but several people had a word with Malcolm Hardee – who ran the gig and who had a propensity for pulling in the most outrageous acts he could manage – and said they weren't sure he should be booking the woman.

## 6. *Chris Lynam*

Chris looked like a malevolent elfin teenager with a huge mass of dark backcombed hair, eyeliner and the general demeanour of someone who was out of control. Some of his act consisted of eating a bar of chocolate by smearing it all over his face or simply abusing the audience as if he was a pissed tramp. His pièce de résistance, however, was shoving a firework up his arse, setting fire to it and standing looking at the audience with a cheeky grin whilst the firework disgorged white hot flames into the air. Yes, I think he did burn his bum a few times, but people loved it. I remember working with him at a pub in Wandsworth, and for some reason he threw a shoe into the audience and by accident it hit a woman on the head and caused copious bleeding. Made a change, I suppose, to reverse the process . . . and have the act chuck things at the audience.

## Performance Poets

It may be hard to believe now, but on the early comedy circuit, performance poets were big news. Many stand-ups started as poets and then switched to pure stand-up, among them Mark Lamarr and Phill Jupitus. Jenny Eclair also started with a bit of poetry; so did the sharp-as-a-knife Mandy Knight, whose poetry was dark, enormously funny and beautifully put together, as was she.

Then, as the circuit grew and became more stand-up orientated, and as bigger, more commercial clubs began to spring up in Central London, like Jongleurs and the Comedy Store, the fringe elements of alternative comedy started to fade away.

John Hegley seems to be the only comedy performance poet who is still going strong, and thank God for that, because it would be morally wrong if he disappeared. If you are a comedy performance poet who is still happily performing and are miffed that I have only mentioned John Hegley, please feel free to write to me and have a right go.

Many acts on the comedy circuit in the early days had silly names, myself included (The Sea Monster). This was not just because they liked having a silly name, it was because many were on the dole and wanted to hide their identity, so they weren't taxed on the extra quids they earned for performing. Legend has it that one performer was called into the dole office and told, 'Look, I saw you on television last night, so it seems unlikely that in the future you will be able to draw state benefits.' He considered himself told.

The weird and wonderful venues flourished, stewarded by the equally weird and wonderful. I remember one club run by Tony Allen, a towering, grizzled figure on the circuit for a while who many people named 'The Godfather of Alternative Comedy'. Tony's club was in an old church in Notting Hill and used to get quite an ethnically mixed audience, unusual since most comedy clubs tended to be relentlessly white.

I did the club one night and was heading to my car, always alert for potential danger, when I heard a roar behind me. I looked round to see a massive black guy running up the street towards me gesticulating wildly and shouting. Oh shit, I thought. Is it going to be a robbery or a sexual assault? There was no point in running as he was legging it up the street at the speed of light. My hands closed round my car keys instinctively as I planned to poke him in the eye if he started anything. Pathetic, really – he was so big I would have needed a bloody ladder. So I just stood there and awaited my fate.

He skidded up to me, patted me on the back and said, 'Well done, you were brilliant tonight.'

So my innate racism was finally revealed and I felt ashamed that I had just assumed he was going to do me harm. Still, it taught me another lesson about London's inhabitants. They are often not what they seem.

## North and South

Given that it is split by a river, I suppose it was inevitable that rivalry would develop between Norf and Sarf Londoners. And indeed it has, to the point that it became a huge cliché for a while that black-cab drivers legendarily would not go south of the river after a cut-off point at night, for fear of the crime-ridden alleys full of murderers and muggers. South Londoners think North Londoners are stuck-up nobheads, whereas North Londoners think themselves more sophisticated and intelligent. North Londoners think South Londoners are rough as old boots and chavvy (I hate that word so much), whereas we South Londoners see ourselves as edgy and interesting.

Who is right? Well, it's completely dependent on where you live. And let's face it, no one outside London gives a toss. As someone who was born in South London and returned there aged twenty to work in Camberwell, I am shot through with loyalty to the Sarf. It's less crowded, there are more green open spaces and a more mixed, chilled-out and generally more attractive community.

North London never has anywhere to park and North Londoners think they're great. Well, someone has to.

But it has to be said that the vast majority of comedy clubs were and are in North London, with a smattering of slightly grubby ones down South. I didn't mind that, as I like grubby. And having lived North of the river for a bit and never being able to park less than half a mile away from my flat, I felt the pull of the South in my heart almost from the kick-off and returned relieved and ecstatic a year or so later.

## The 'C' word

'Cunt' was a forbidden word in the early days of the circuit. When alternative comedy developed away from the traditional circuit, the unspoken (but known by everyone) rules discouraged racist or anti-women jokes; the 'C' word was considered to be offensive towards women.

My friend Alan Davies remembers it as being a real taboo in the early days, and Mark Kelly recalls a comic called Tony Morewood being one of the first to bring it back into the fold – in reference to a member of the audience. From this point it seems the 'C' word was reclaimed by various comics, most of them men, ironically, until it began to enter the arena of words that were once offensive, but now have lost their bite.

It seems though that it has not quite been rehabilitated, and perhaps still needs to be said by Holly Willoughby on *This Morning* or someone on *Springwatch*, maybe, before it completely loses its bite. I have mixed feelings towards the dear old 'C' word. I know it can be offensive to women, but there's nothing quite like the primitive ejection of it into the universe when one is at the height of anger or frustration; nothing else quite replaces it. So, what I'm really saying is I'm a hypocrite. I don't think people should use it, but I do.

As the comedy circuit developed and grew, the commercial possibilities on offer caused the more fringey acts to drop off the edges. Clubs started to open that could be real money-making business opportunities for hard-nosed promoters, rather than the idiosyncratic comedy wannabes who had hitherto run clubs. So the Comedy Store and Jongleurs were born and the small, odd clubs started to disappear along with the small, odd acts.

And, with the new clubs came new and different types of audiences. From your stereotypical beard-strokers ('and that was just the women,' many comics I know would have remarked) suddenly there were audiences from outside Town who didn't have an allotment or a solar panel to their name. They wanted a GOOD NIGHT OUT and they weren't prepared to put up with any polemical nonsense, comedy mime or poems about the political sitch in Peru. They wanted clever, slick stand-ups with a joke rate to equal Mr B. Connolly's, and they were ruthless in their disdain of the gentle drama-school wordsmith.

There was an influx of Irish blokes onto the London

circuit when they realised they could actually earn a living. London said hello to Sean Hughes, Michael Redmond, Dylan Moran, Patrick Kielty and many others. The comedy circuit in America seemed to be faltering slightly too, and that meant that Bill Hicks, Emo Philips, Steven Wright, Will Durst and Dennis Leary all ventured across the Atlantic to have a crack at the English.

The comedy circuit in America sounds far more hierarchical than it is over here. (I've never been.) Comics have definitive places on a bill and have to work their way up the ladder to be 'the closing act' who earns more than the rest. In London it was different in the early days. There was no such thing as 'Top of the Bill'. Most bills at London clubs in the mid-eighties were interchangeable. However, things started to change as audiences began turning up to see particular acts. My friend Mark tells me that at 'new material' nights, audience members would ask if certain comics like myself were on. God bless him, he had to say that or I would have chinned him.

For a long time, everything was centred in London, and although there were one or two far-flung outposts of comedy, like a tiny club in Bungay in Suffolk run by Malcolm Hardee, all comedy was Londoncentric.

Of course this has changed enormously since I started; now every town and city has its comedy club, while Jongleurs has spread like a virus round the entire country.

### The Tunnel Club

The Tunnel Club was run by the inimitable and chaotic Malcolm Hardee whose catchphrase 'Oi oi!' would preface any interaction he would have with the audience. He would shamble onto the stage looking like a cross between a tramp, Frank Carson and a little boy with Eric Morecambe-type glasses. The audience absolutely loved him and didn't care that he did the same material week in and week out, to the point that they could repeat it along with him.

Whenever an act was on who was struggling, the cry would go up from the scary heckly bit at the back on the right-hand side . . . 'Malcolm!' . . . and if it started to build and everyone started shouting Malcolm's name, he would have to come back on and shoo off whichever poor sod was doing his best against a tide of derision and no laughs.

Malcolm's other catchphrase was 'Fuck it', which he would liberally sprinkle throughout his compering. Malcolm would often resort to getting his genitalia out for a laugh and occasionally would place a pair of glasses on the top of his bollocks – his impersonation of General De Gaulle, and an unsettlingly accurate one at that. People always said he had the longest bollocks on the circuit (it's not like there were loads of other pairs of bollocks on display), and although there was never actually a competition to find out the truth of this statement, I think they were probably right.

The Tunnel Club was the modern equivalent for comedians of the Roman Coliseum. If you got the thumbs-down from the audience, you were dead – no empathy, no support, you just had to get off. As you made your way to the stage, you could often hear members of the audience shouting, 'Crucify her!' or similarly reassuring supportive comments, and it did really feel like you were being fed to a baying mob.

On the whole, it was a non-violent place and you were reasonably safe apart from a bruised ego, but one incident there heralded the beginning of the end. The female half of a double act called Clarence and Joy Pickles was hit in the face by a heavy plastic beer glass and cut quite badly. Following this, comics were urged by Arthur Smith to boycott the Tunnel. Quite a few did, and it was a while before things got back to normal.

All this only increased the Tunnel's reputation as a scary gig.

One night, an American comic juggler – you're in a coma already, I know – attempted to involve the audience in his act by throwing his skittles (or whatever they're called) into the crowd, to be returned when he asked. He soon discovered to his cost that the Tunnel audience didn't play that game, and one was aimed back at him with the ferocity of an Olympic javelin-thrower, whistling at great speed past his head and causing the audience to send up a massive, bloodthirsty cheer. However, as the next one sailed towards him with breathtaking acceleration, he actually managed a body swerve and caught it. Suddenly the audience loved him and he could do no wrong and went on to storm it.

It was because of the completely arbitrary nature of the punters at the Tunnel that most comics feared its power. Add to that a clever audience whose ability to place a well-honed heckle was second to none, and you did face true humiliation. However, if you got through it, the rewards to your self-esteem were tremendous and you felt like a hero.

My approach was to step on stage and just stand staring at the audience while they roared, railed and abused me at the top of their voices. Eventually they would get bored, and as the noise died down I would launch into my set at a hundred miles an hour and pray. I must have done the Tunnel four or five times and am proud to report I have an unblemished record and was never booed off.

However, to wheel out a cliché, all good things must come to an end, and the Tunnel did not last. Details are sketchy in my head, but there was a police raid following a stabbing in the car park, and the Tunnel was forced to close. My friend Mark remembers looking back over his shoulder as he left during the chaos of the raid, to see Malcolm stark naked on stage holding a dog on a lead which was trying to bite him on the bollocks. A fitting image, I feel.

## The Comedy Café

The Comedy Café was our refuge after shows. It was a place where we could drink, hide and chew over the night's stand-up, as all the comics who met there had come from every end of London to relax and get a bit pissed. Initially the room above the club itself, in Rivington Street just on the edge of the City, was slightly bare, but Noel Faulkner, the endlessly generous and sweet overseer of the club, allowed us to do pretty much what we wanted to the place to make it more homely. We got hold of a few grotty old settees and Alan Davies tells me I forked out for a pool table, although I don't remember this, and it became a little private club for us to meet at the end of a Friday and Saturday night.

The core group was myself, Alan Davies, Mark Lamarr, Andy Linden, Keith Dover, Jim Miller (aka James Macabre), Hattie Hayridge (Holly from *Red Dwarf* to you), Simon Clayton, John Gordillo and Andre Vincent, plus an ever-changing cast-list of comics and performers – Ross Noble and Jools Holland among them. I wasn't particularly young and sprightly then as I hadn't started stand-up until I was thirty, but Alan Davies, looking back, can't believe how young the core group were, mainly in their early twenties. Alan remembers going on at the Comedy Café gig one night just after Mark Lamarr, and a bloke in his forties with a couple of similarly aged mates saying very loudly to them, 'How old's this one?'

We also used the Comedy Café room during the World Cup in 1990. Noel got a massive telly in for us and we watched the Germany game there. Alan recalls being slightly miffed that a load of extra comics turned up and all the decent seats were taken when he arrived.

It was, of course, the semi-final in which Gazza was booked and cried, and Waddle and Pearce missed their penalties. Huge depression and England's inability to deliver the killer blow has been repeated endlessly throughout many World and European Cups.

We were young, we were attractive (ish) and we had enormously good fun – and I think about those days as a time of mega-laughs, a few fights and making really good friendships.

# My Best and Worst Comedy Clubs

It was strange not being a nurse any more and having virtually no responsibility apart from writing jokes and managing to drag myself out of the house in time for a gig in the evening. At the time there was a thriving comedy circuit in London. Each club had its own, very personal characteristics – to do with the nature of the venue, the type of audience that came there and whether there was a regular compere or not. Here, in no particular order, are a few of my favourites:

# Best Comedy Clubs

## The Chuckle Club

The Chuckle Club was and is run by someone called Eugene Cheese. (I don't think that is his real name!) When I performed there, it was in a pub just off Carnaby Street, which was quite unusual as lots of comedy clubs, apart from big 'uns like the Comedy Store, didn't tend to be in the West End but flung out towards the fringes of mainly North London with a sprinkling East, a few West and hardly any South.

I liked the Chuckle Club because despite the fact that it was quite a small club, Eugene always paid top dollar and was very fair with the door split. The crowd were mainly regulars who had developed an audience personality of welcoming bonhomie so it was always a joy to do.

## The Red Rose

The Red Rose Labour Club in Finsbury Park in North London always felt to me like a spiritual home of some sort. Compered by Ivor Dembina, who was my flatmate for a while, it had a left-wing feel. Although it's possible with hindsight that I have imposed such a trait, and that the audience didn't give a toss – they just wanted some good entertainment. It was run by

Joe, a lovely Irishman who was into comedy and very happy to have us all there.

I had some great nights and some fairly appalling nights there, which is par for the course.

We also tried to start up a Comics' Union there. The fundamental problem, of course, with doing that is that comics tend to be loners who don't naturally fit into a unionised environment. However, Ivor and I sent out a message and were hugely impressed that more than 150 people turned up at the first meeting. We had called it mainly because we felt that some clubs were discriminating against less experienced comics and paying them much less than other comics.

As you can imagine, a room full of that many comics was quite something to behold and there was much heckling (well, how often did *we* get the chance?) and pissing about.

At the initial meeting, various issues were discussed and it was agreed that we would meet a month later, and that Ivor and I would do some groundwork to start sorting some of the problems.

Of course at the next meeting there were only thirty comics and at the following about twelve, so the Comics' Union I'm afraid went the way of many altruistic projects, under the heading of Just Can't Be Arsed.

The other disappointment I had at the Red Rose was one Christmas Eve when I parked right outside, intending to do a gig and then drive straight on to my parents' for Christmas in Shropshire. During the gig someone smashed the car window and nicked all my presents which I'D VERY STUPIDLY LEFT ON THE BACK SEAT. Christmas cheer evaporated out of me immediately and I did hold it against the Red Rose for quite some time. Although I hope they liked the satin thong I'd got my dad for Christmas.

## CAST Comedy Clubs

CAST was a left-wing organisation which ran comedy gigs at various venues round London including the Hackney Empire. They put on an eclectic mix of performers, ranging from a South African woman in her sixties called Terri who did paper-tearing, to hard-nosed old lefties who slagged the government with every last fibre of their being. The main reason I liked them was because of the couple who ran them, Claire and Roland Muldoon. Roland was a bearded Cap'n Birdseye-type, full of bonhomie and humour, and Claire, a witty, straight-talking feminist.

I still try to keep in touch with them and do gigs for them when I can. In fact, I recently went to the small village in which they live in the wilds of Buckinghamshire to do some stand-up in the village hall. I had been dubious about it because the weather forecast predicted very heavy snow, and I didn't particularly want to get stuck on the motorway and have to eat my own leg while I froze to death. I mooted this idea with Claire, who sounded so bereft that I was considering not coming, that I steeled myself and got in the car.

The gig itself was a laugh, a lot of pissed villagers shouting, heckling and enjoying themselves. My dressing room was the disabled toilet, which was perfectly all right and even had a chair if I put the lid down.

I came out of the show to face bitter cold and thought I'd better get back to London as quickly as I could. I hit the motorway twenty minutes later and within seconds it had started to snow. Because it was so cold the heavy snow settled immediately and I was forced to slow down to ten miles an hour because I couldn't see a bloody thing, owing to what I think is called a white-out. One's driving skills go out of the window on these occasions and I immediately started driving very badly. I'm sure I was straddling two lanes as I couldn't see the road.

Eventually I settled in behind a massive lorry and

kept on his tail, limping into London where the snow had melted immediately, due probably to the fact that London is such an evil place, and arrived home four hours later. Yes, cheers, Claire.

## New Material Nights

New material nights were a good example of comics cooperating and working together. Originally they started in a pub just off Tottenham Court Road and were an opportunity for comics to try out new stuff they had written. It's hard because on its first outing, new material is so obviously new that if you do it at a booked show you have fifteen minutes of polished, funny, well-tested stuff with five minutes of absolute crap in the middle.

The new material nights gave us a chance to socialise, try stuff and hopefully give the audience what they wanted. We always employed a proper compere and paid them, so that at least if all our bits were really shit, the audience got some good jokes out of them.

Comics who did new material nights were Jim Tavaré, James Macabre, Hattie Hayridge, Simon Munnery, Stewart Lee, Mark Thomas, Alan Davies, Ivor Dembina, Patrick Marber and many others. We eventually moved to a more permanent home in Islington and would do the gig then all drift along the road to Pizza Express for some laughs, arguments and occasional bad behaviour.

### Screaming Blue Murder at the Leather Bottle

The Leather Bottle is in South-West London, and Screaming Blue Murder was run by two delightful brothers called Pete and Phil. The regular compere was Eddie Izzard, who had come into his own after what some people on the comedy circuit considered to be a shaky start. But here he was in his element, and his surreal flights of fancy lifted the audience to dizzy heights of laughter. Those of us who were waiting to go on split our thoughts between marvelling at Eddie's skill and hoping the determinedly pro-Eddie audience would like us too.

## Worst Comedy Clubs

### The Bearcat

James and Graham, the lovely guys who run the Bearcat Club, which was housed in a lovely little pub in Twickenham, will kill me for putting their club into my least favourite league. It has absolutely nothing to do with them: I was, and still am, very fond of them. They never had a compere as such. James would stand in front of a record deck playing seventies disco hits between the acts while people went to the bar, and one would either step on stage just after 'It's Raining Men' or 'I Will Survive'. Sometimes I felt I myself only very narrowly survived.

It had to do with the audience who went there. I have no idea why this should be, but I can't remember ever having a gig that I truly enjoyed at the Bearcat. There always seemed to be someone in the audience who *really* didn't like me. Fair enough – I accept that the whole world can't like me or find me funny – but when the abuse came, as it did from time to time, I never felt the rest of the audience were that bothered. All right then, let the narky cow have it, was what I imagined them to be thinking.

My worst night there was a New Year's Eve gig. I've never been that keen on the forced jollity-cum-psycho-pissedness of New Year's Eve when we're all supposed to be having a brilliant time despite the fact that at least half of us aren't.

It should have been a great night, but there had been some industrial-strength drinking going on, and by the time I stepped on stage, the atmosphere wasn't great. Alcohol-induced possibilities filled the air and they'd already been having a right old heckle at the other acts. There was quite a lot of 'Fuck off, you fat lesbian' which, to be honest, had become so familiar over the years that it didn't bother me any more. Then someone shouted out something along the lines of, 'Piss off, you're shit.' I did one of my put-downs, probably about halfway along the continuum strength-wise. Normally it would get a laugh, but they just looked at me like I was a really horrible person.

At that point I knew I had lost them. Although not many people who perform take a huge amount of notice of where they appear on the bill, if you are on last, the audience tends to think you are the headline act and therefore the best. Well, I was dying on my arse and everything I tried to do to counteract it seemed to have the effect of a funeral bell tolling. Absolutely nothing worked. I managed to stagger through to the end of my set without the audience actually dealing the final blow, but came off feeling deflated, angry with myself and really pissed off. And A Happy New Year to me.

**The Cartoon in Clapham**
The Cartoon was a rowdy pub in Clapham where there was a comedy club for a while. Perhaps it was just bad luck, but every time I went there, it seemed someone was either vomiting over their table, or there was a

fight, or a group of stag-night types who wanted to fire a heat-seeking missile of abuse at me. I tried not to perform there too often.

It would be morally wrong to finish this chapter without including a short-list of my own ill-judged remarks while on stage:

1. At a pro-abortion benefit, I made a (made up!) joke about my boyfriend coming to see me, just after I'd had a termination and to cheer me up, bringing a bag of jelly babies.

2. I told a twelve-year-old boy in the front row of a gig, who was heckling me, to fuck off. Which obviously didn't go down a treat with his mum and dad.

3. I berated a guy walking across in front of me who subsequently went to the bar, bought a pint of lager and came back and chucked it over me.

4. I told a room full of businessmen that they were all wankers (they were), but it finished my evening pretty sharpish.

5. At a student gig I threw a bun, which had been thrown at me, back in the direction of the thrower and it hit some poor innocent woman in the eye.

For these, and the thousand other dodgy pieces of behaviour I have indulged in and subsequently repressed, I am well and truly regretful.

# On Tour (or In a Car for Hours)

Many comedians believe touring to be a necessary evil, but I really love it. It's self-contained, straightforward, and when a night's finished it's finished and there's no hangover from it unless you have died on your arse – but a few drinks soon sorts that out.

I have toured many times over the last twenty years, and each town seems to have its own particular characteristics. Rather than laboriously detail each tour, it's perhaps best to give you an overall impression of touring and then list towns I've been to which have had a major impression.

My touring life is divided into two sections: pre-children and after-children. Before I got married and had kids I was free to tour wherever I wanted and for however long I wanted to, which meant that I could be away for several days and do a tour that progressed in a logical way round the country. Well I say that, but Off the Kerb, which is the company I tour with, are famous for throwing you the occasional googly by putting you on in Aberdeen one night, Southampton the next and then Glasgow the next. This means you criss-cross the country quite a few times, and if you don't like sitting in cars you're in trouble.

For me, the most important requirements of sitting in a car for ages are good companions, a good driver, good radio and/or music, and lots of sweets. Once all these are in place, on the whole things are OK. The only problem after that is the motorways. These grind to a halt with alarming regularity, but I have to say that not once have I arrived late for a show, so we have obviously always been sensibly grown up in setting off in plenty of time, although there have been a few skin-of-our-teeth moments.

**Support Acts**
I toured firstly with my friend Jeff Green for a number of years until he became worthy of tours in his own

right, and I was sad to see him go. I then toured for a while with Richard Morton, who was always great to be with. Richard is such a lovable guy, so helpful, friendly and sweet-natured, he almost makes me feel guilty for existing. He's a Geordie, but an atypical one given that he is small and slim and unmacho. He was unerringly cheerful when we toured briefly, and believe you me, unerringly cheerful isn't the default position of most comedians.

Richard did stand-up and comedy songs, and can be spotted in the background in a club in that wonderful series *Our Friends in the North*. He also happens to have the same name as an opera singer and was booked to do a gig at the Sherman Theatre near Cardiff once. However, the audience were expecting the opera singer – and when Richard kicked off with, 'My daddy was a sperm bank, he came on my account . . .' almost the entire audience got up and left.

I have finally ended up with Andy Robinson, with whom I still tour. He is an absolute joy to work with, since he's self-deprecating, generous, very funny and relaxed – and his cynical attitude towards the business is very similar to mine.

We have such good fun when we're touring because we get on so well. We like the same kind of music so there are never any arguments in the car about what we have on (Elvis Costello, Morrissey, Nick Cave-type stuff). However, Andy is a big Elvis Presley fan and I'm afraid I draw the line at The King because I am one of those sad people who prefer his later stuff like 'Suspicious Minds' and 'The Wonder of You', which I think proper Elvis fans consider to be not very good. My main attitude towards Elvis Presley, by the way, is that he was essentially a simple country lad who just happened to be enormously good-looking and a brilliant singer, and who was then sucked into the world of showbiz and gradually chewed up in the most painful and visible sort of way.

Many comics have included either an Elvis fat joke or a dying-on-the-toilet joke in their set but I always felt pity for him – the evidence of his decline was there for all to see as he gained weight through what I presume was comfort-eating born out of his isolation. Elvis fans, if I've got this wrong, please let me know.

That's the problem with excess eating . . . IT SHOWS. So although alcoholics and heroin addicts can maintain their svelte figures, big eaters can't, and piss-taking will inevitably occur. Ditto Michael Jackson with his unearthly metamorphosis from beautiful boy into alienated alien. I'm sure the added pressures of being global stars just compounded their emotional confusion.

God forbid I should ever have to tour with one of what I tend to think of as 'The Ambitious Boys'. There are plenty of these around. Clever, career-minded, pushy little buggers whose only thought is for their own advancement. Bloody good luck to 'em but they're not my cup of tea to spend time with, because you feel you are in a constant battle for airtime with them.

## Tour Managers

As well as a so-called 'support act', one always has a tour manager. He or she drives, liaises with the theatre staff, fights off the adoring fans (yes, that's never happened), marshals any press people and generally is available for weird showbiz requests should you have a sudden urge for pheasant testicles in batter at 2 a.m. on a wet Tuesday in Norwich. I hope I am not a whim-laden sort of performer, by the way, and have always done my best to keep to a minimum these sorts of mad demands. I think the most I've ever managed is some fags or a packet of Haribos. Over the years my tour managers have been Mark, John, Jez and Grazio, thankfully none of them behaving hideously badly. (Apart from on a few occasions.)

Being a tour manager involves a lot of different skills and at times it's very boring. First of all there's a huge amount of driving involved. You're the first one to start in the morning and the last one to get home to bed once you've dropped everyone off.

Mark was tour manager, if I remember rightly, for one and a half tours. He was dead easygoing, which is essential, didn't force his musical tastes on us and did his job efficiently and with good grace. One major worry was that on the second leg of touring he had rather a lot of points on his licence for speeding, and if he picked up another three that would have pushed him over and made him ineligible to drive, so there were a few sharp intakes of breath on various journeys but thankfully, we never crossed the point of no return.

John had worked in security before he began tour managing for me and was quite big and scary-looking; this is a bonus, because it puts some people off approaching you even before any trouble has started. Apparently, he looks like David Platt, the footballer, because someone once came up to us when we were in the street to ask for an autograph and I found myself just assuming (Bighead Brand) that this guy was approaching me. As I stuck my hand out to take the pen, he said, 'No, I want David Platt's,' making me feel very small and vain and giving us a good laugh at the same time.

John never felt the need to punch anyone, for which I'm eternally grateful. He just stood there and glowered at them, and nine times out of ten that was all it took.

Jez was a mate of mine, who took over on a tour when John couldn't do it any more – and God bless him, he had only just passed his driving test, so was somewhat wobbly on the finer details. We had a couple of hair-raising moments on roundabouts, but on the whole managed pretty well. It was slightly difficult at times because we were mates and I don't like asking anyone to do anything, particularly a friend, but we muddled through and sorted stuff out. However, Jez was great to work with because I knew him so well. He had a brilliant comic brain and timing, and I often thought he should be getting up on stage too.

Grazio is an utterly charming, very helpful and sweet-tempered man who has also toured with the likes of Lee Evans and Michael McIntyre. He is a completely soothing person to travel with, is very helpful, and his anticipatory skills are nothing short of miraculous. He is reliable and calm and in short, probably the perfect tour manager; in fact, he would win an award for tour managing, should there be such a thing.

### 'Getting Your Head Down'

When I first started touring, the tour dates tended to be continuous, one date after another with a break of one or two days during which to recover before setting off again. Initially, in the early days one of us comics would drive and we would be booked into cheap B&Bs with suspicious couples eyeing us up over breakfast wondering why we were under ninety years of age.

As the old career progressed, the B&Bs metamorphosed into cheapish hotels which could be terrifying. I remember staying in a particularly scary hotel in Liverpool one night. I arrived at the door of my room, having staggered up there from the bar, to discover that it had been kicked in the night before and had had a piece of hardboard nailed, very badly, over it. In the room next door, a loud argument was going on between two blokes, with the occasional sound of smashing glass or splintering wood. Pushing a chest of drawers against the door, I lay on the bed with all my clothes on and eschewed the communal toilet in the hall in favour of weeing in the sink.

When the tours were longer and more lucrative, we

found ourselves in what I would consider to be posh hotels, great big ones in town where you could have breakfast in your room, raid the minibar and hang your clothes up on the trouser press for want of a better thing to do with them if you were a lady.

I used to lie on the bed flicking through the hundreds of channels on the telly, necking a lager and thinking, How could I ever get bored with this?

But the weird thing is, you do eventually. After seeing the inside of hundreds of hotel rooms, they do begin to merge into one, and you long for the quirkiness of your own place with all the familiar crap in it. It's even worse when you have a family you can't go home to see. This was why, after I'd had children, I would go home every night after a gig and start out anew every day. This obviously made days longer and tours harder, and meant that the distance I was prepared to go shrank a bit, but I would far rather have done that than stay away for days on end.

## At Last – Trying To Make Them Laugh

Once you arrive at a theatre for a gig, normally two hours or so before it's due to start, you explore your dressing room. These range from sumptuous big rooms with the clichéd mirrors with light bulbs round them and posh sofas, to tiny, suspicious-smelling hovels with one small settee that looks as if an incontinent tramp has been sleeping on it for a fortnight. You then have to do the obligatory sound check, which involves inter-acting with the techies at the theatre – again a huge range of individuals, from cheery blokes who bung the kettle on and are happy to furnish you with local know-ledge, to teenagers covered in heavy-metal tattoos who can barely look at you, let alone manage anything approaching a word. It is a huge joy when people are friendly and welcoming. Sadly, some of them decide in advance that you are a showbiz twat and go out of their way to demonstrate this. As someone who goes out of *my* way to be unerringly polite and friendly, I find this a complete pain in the arse.

After the sound check, there is quite a lot of sitting down and talking bollocks until the show starts. I have found I really need this time to get into gear for the show. I don't get as nervous as I used to (butterflies for a week before a gig), but there are certain circum-stances which are more conducive to being in the right mood for a gig. Firstly, I'm not good at socialising before I do a show as my thoughts are on what's coming up, rather than chatting to a local journalist about how I got into comedy. It's also nice to be somewhere private.

I once did a benefit and discovered my dressing room was the same room as the green room for friends, family and press with a makeshift bar, and Andy and I sat in the corner trying to write out our set-list. The changing facilities were a handily placed screen in the corner of the room, and someone peeking round it just as I was taking my trousers off was the last flipping straw.

I tend to write my set out three times, don't ask me why, I've forgotten by now. I also stick some prompt notes on a speaker in front of the mic more as a security blanket rather than actually needing it.

As 'show time' approaches, various announcements come through on the relay in the dressing room, counting you down. My favourites are always the old-fashioned stage managers who say things like, 'Tonight's concert will begin in fifteen minutes.' I always want to run round and shout, 'It's not a bleeding concert, it's a comedy show.'

Andy always goes on first. I usually make an announcement from a mic backstage to introduce him, warning the punters that the show will be quite rude – so if they don't like swearing, they'd better fuck off now. Audiences who tut at this tend not to laugh very much, as you can imagine. After that, I stand backstage and watch the first five minutes to get a flavour of what the audience is like. Surely, you're thinking, an audience is an audience is an audience – but you're wrong. There are so many subtle (and unsubtle) differences in the way that audiences behave. The day of the week makes a difference, the weather, the time of year, the size of the theatre – lots of things like that. Also, if there are hecklers, it's useful to know what they've said to Andy so I can pick up on it later.

Once on stage, I kick off with a line that I know works, just to make sure they're not going to hate me. Again, levels of laughter are quite subtle and I can always tell if they're not quite there. At this point I might change my plan to improvise a bit of local stuff and replace it with some tried and tested material just to really get them going before I push off into the unknown. However, if it's all gone well so far, I'll do some stuff on local news. I always buy a local paper and scan it in the dead zone between sound check and performance. Local papers give you a good idea of what local concerns are, and sometimes in predominantly rural areas I find stuff that wouldn't even get a look-in in our *South London Press*. In Hay-on-Wye in Wales, one year at the Literary Festival, I found a story on the front page, *Hanging Basket Stolen*, which struck me as so sweet.

Audiences seem to really like you talking about their home territory and it usually elicits some responses from them and encourages them to join in, until it feels like they are really involved. On several occasions, people in the audience have actually featured in some of the stories and joined in on enlarging on the story itself. The rest of the audience loves this and it's so great when it happens.

Major concerns round the country seem to be crime, parking and rubbish. The other bit of the paper I use a lot is the letters page, on which complaints about dog poo and petty crime feature heavily. The review of the papers can last anything from two minutes to fifteen depending on how well it goes. In Brecon once, I mentioned a story about a minor earthquake and an interview with a woman who'd said that when she'd heard the earthquake, she'd assumed it was her Labrador wagging his tail against the side of the bath. Of course, several people knew her!

It's quite interesting how the amount of material one does in a show can expand enormously or concertina down into almost half the length, depending on how relaxed you are and how responsive the audience is.

I had a particularly difficult gig at the Hammersmith Apollo one night which was being filmed for TV. For some reason, I have always felt that the audience at the Apollo were not my natural constituency and so I always found it a bit of a struggle. But on this particular day, it was even more difficult because my dear, lovely grandma Maisie had died the night before and I was feeling very sad and slightly out of touch with reality. Maybe I shouldn't have gone ahead with it, but I thought once I got on stage I could just work my way through on automatic pilot. I had prepared forty minutes of material, which is what they wanted but, given that the audience seemed a bit cold and I felt like I was on another planet, for some reason my set shrank down to twenty minutes because I rushed it and pruned all the excess, which one normally includes when one is relaxed and on a roll. Well, there was a slight hiatus and I marched off stage feeling defeated. The poor compere, Russell Howard, who'd expected me to be on for another twenty minutes, was in the lav so the audience was treated to an empty stage while someone rushed round in a panic trying to find him.

The upshot of this was that the production company asked me to come back two days later and do some more material, as the pathetic amount I'd produced was not enough for my allotted slot on telly.

Knowing that all my material had been used up, this

meant that the material I'd have to do two days later would all have to be new stuff. This was terrifying, because normally new material takes at least five live shows to work in and to give you the chance to dump stuff which is crap. I didn't have the luxury of this time available so I had to write some stuff and do it for the very first time in front of an audience of 3,000 people whilst being filmed for telly. What a fucking nightmare. So off I went two days later to the theatre and just trotted it out to the best of my ability. Lenny Henry was compering, the audience was up for a good night and thank God, on the whole the material worked. It didn't storm it, but I would never have expected it first time out and I was just relieved that they didn't stare at me for fifteen minutes without laughing.

One concept comics are very familiar with is that of 'getting on a roll'. This is when the audience seems to laugh continuously throughout the whole performance, and as the laugh dies down from one joke or remark it starts to build up for the next bit. Not only do they laugh at punch lines, they laugh at the build-up to jokes as well. It's a glorious thing to be a performer in a show like that. It doesn't happen all the time and on many occasions you get a sort of stop/start response to your jokes. Laugh-silence-laugh-silence is the pattern, and once it's been set up it's hard to break. 'I never really got on a roll,' is the lament of many a comic at a difficult gig.

Encores are always lovely too, but it's important not to expect them. There's nothing better as you walk off stage than to hear huge applause, and then the shouts start to build gradually for 'More!' until they become a roar and feet are stamped too, and it's so great to go back on and bask in it. It doesn't always happen, but I suppose it is always the aim of the comic to get as many encores as possible. I think Billy Connolly is the King of the Multiple Encore. The most I've had is three.

# Enormously Subjective Countrywide Comedy Guide

I discovered information about each town I performed in by reading the *Rough Guide to Great Britain*, and during the gig I would tell the audience, 'Well, the Fucking Rough Guide in your case.' Worked every time!

**Basingstoke**
Very hung over after a night in Hastings the night before. Had to stare straight in front of me on stage to avoid being sick.

## Bedford

Bedford has a delightful entry in the *Rough Guide to England* which states, *The town need not detain you*. I'm sure the people of Bedford are mighty impressed by that.

My favourite night at Bedford involved the sound and lighting man being quite pissed and falling over onto his desk, cutting the sound and lights at the same time. It was a real *Carrie* moment and I was expecting a bucket of blood on my head at any second. As well as this, a woman in the audience asked me to sign one of her bosoms: something that has never happened before or indeed since. She informed me that she wanted to show it to her husband.

'Where's he tonight then?' I asked.

'In the nick,' came her reply.

## Birmingham

Birmingham is always a joy. People are friendly, welcoming and happy to see you. It's always lovely to get a really big cheer when you come on, with no holds barred. Many towns and cities withhold their initial reaction until they've had a look at the goods.

Birmingham is also under the jurisdiction of King Jasper Carrott who, every year, does a huge show at the

NEC (12,000 seats – ooer!) There is normally a cavalcade of interesting stars and I worked with Jack Dee, Dame Edna, Manfred Mann and some sweeties off *The X Factor*. Someone attempted a rather over-intimate massage to relax me before the show (he was actually a professional masseur), and I left the massage area as soon as was humanly possible.

## Brighton

Vibrant, cool and good fun. The Dome in Brighton is the only time a rather disturbed punter found their way back stage and demanded to be put on the show to do five minutes. Typically, John the tour manager was right over the other side of the building, but I managed to phone someone called Joe from Off the Kerb and leave a message. Atypically, Joe called me back just at a critical moment when this bloke's face was about an inch away from mine. Not only that, he'd obviously not realised quite how disturbed this guy was and was laughing uproariously at the end of the phone, saying, 'Shall we give him five minutes? Do you think he's any good?' I was terrified that the intruder would hear what he was saying and deck me, but thankfully, at that moment John appeared behind me and our friend was 'escorted from the premises', as the euphemism goes.

A slightly more pleasant experience involved Sir Ian McKellen, with whom I took part in a benefit at the Dome. I was sitting at the mirror in the dressing room backcombing my hair to produce The Bride of Frankenstein look, which I loved in the eighties, and Sir Ian went past. Spotting me doing my hair, he said, 'Ooh, can I do that?'

And he did – the one and only time I've ever had an acting legend sort my hair out for me.

## Bristol

I love Bristol. One of my first big gigs was in a venue called the Bierkeller, which was obviously a music venue. The dressing room contained one of those wrecked, scuzzy settees I have already mentioned, and the stage was carpeted and looked well manky. It was. When I stepped on it my feet stuck to it as if they had been glued and each step towards the mic was accompanied by a tearing sound as I tried to lift my foot off the carpet. The audience was enthusiastic and drunk.

You can tell how long ago it was because I had some material about the Chippendales, the delightful male dancers/strippers who were flavour of the month back in the early nineties. As I progressed through my little five-minute routine on the Chippendales, a voice heckled from the back in a perfect West Country accent: 'They're all queer, they are.' Well, there were still a few steadfast pockets of homophobia round the country.

'How do you know that?' I asked.

The reply came, again in that gorgeous accent. 'I 'eard it down the Colston 'All.'

The Colston Hall was a venue a little distance away that was bigger and I hadn't quite progressed to it by that point. But I was interested in the fact that it seemed to be the fount of all knowledge on sexuality. Years later, I actually made it to the Colston Hall and related this event to the audience, asking them, 'How do you know?'

A voice floated back across the crowd, 'We just do.'

## Bromsgrove

Bromsgrove is a little town lying just outside Birmingham. I came out of the dressing room to stand outside on the pavement just as three police cars, sirens blaring, swept up. I immediately, of course, thought they were after me. They weren't. One of the theatre staff had laid into a female relative outside the stage door. A very surreal night indeed.

## Cambridge

Oooh, posh as you like in Cambridge, comrades. Tried to get the audience to guess what my 'wife leader' was. (It's a woven stick with an elasticated end to attach to your wife's finger and lead her round by, used in the Caribbean 300 years ago.) Fantastic woman in front row threw out the suggestion, 'Is it a cassava juice extractor?' Blimey, what sort of kitchen shops do you have in Cambridge?

## Cheltenham

Cheltenham is dead posh, no doubt about that. Performing at the Town Hall is like being in a museum, surrounded as you are by marble busts of various luminaries, giving the whole thing a bit of an historical feel. This doesn't mean that the audience are staid and stuffy, even though they look it a bit, and any trawl I have done through the local papers there has always been good fun, obsessed as they seem to be with parking and dog poo. Oh, the great British sensibilities – you can't beat 'em!

## Derby

Derby seems to me like a bit of a scary old town. The gigs I have done there have always been good, apart from having a bombscare at one all-women's gig from a disgruntled male punter. However, there is a street in Derby which is full of pubs and clubs, all the doors fiercely guarded by bloody massive bouncers in dicky bows and evening jackets. (Always seems so weird to me that they are dressed up posh yet ready to punch your lights out.) After a show one night we went down this particular street to have a Chinese, and just walking down it terrified the life out of me. I take my hat off to anyone who is brave enough to actually go and have a whole night out there.

### Hastings
My home town, where I grew up as a teenager. Always a pleasure to be there, despite receiving a letter in the dressing room once, saying:

> *Dear Miss Brand,*
> *Please do not come back to Hastings again.*
> *Yours faithfully etc etc.*

I recently did a benefit for my nephew's football changing hut which had been burned down, and took the piss out of a bloke's hair in the second row, without realising it was my brother's mother-in-law's bloke.

Note to self: *wear glasses on stage.*

## Ipswich and Norwich

I have put these two cities together, not because they are particularly similar but because they suffer the misfortune of being in an area of the country which, for comedy reasons, is full of interbred people and very flat, and therefore the inhabitants doubtless are regaled endlessly with jokes about cousins marrying, fingers in dykes and being able to see your friends standing fifty miles away. Consequently, I steered well clear of this when I was up there. They didn't seem particularly grateful though.

## Leicester

By the time we hit the brand new pristine council venue in Leicester, the smoking ban had kicked in big time and there were signs everywhere demanding *No Smoking* throughout the venue. It was in Leicester that we experimented with the idea of putting a condom over the smoke alarm. Worked a treat.

## Maidstone

Maidstone, sorry, you had the worst toilets of any theatre I have ever been to, and the dressing room wasn't much better. It seemed rather fitting then that I forgot my smart shoes and had to wear flip-flops on stage instead.

## Manchester

I've performed in Manchester loads of times. The audiences there tend to be cynical, clever and discerning. I made a huge faux pas at the Free Trade Hall once, which interestingly was the scene of Bob Dylan's metamorphosis from acoustic to electronic music, during which a member of the audience called out 'Judas!' I came close to knowing how that felt.

At the time, our tour manager John was doing some security work and had a bulletproof vest in the boot of the car. So for a laugh (how much trouble has that phrase prefaced?) I put the vest on, and when I went on stage, remarked that I was wearing it because we were quite close to the notorious crime area of Moss Side. BIG MISTAKE. The booing started at the back and swept forward in a great tidal wave towards me.

Bloody hell, I thought. I'm going to have to get off now and I've only just come on.

The only thing for it was to apologise, which I did, and it seemed to pour oil on troubled waters. The audience accepted it and I carried on, and getting to the end of the hour, I felt that I had managed to claw the evening back. However, it taught me the lesson that some towns and cities do not like having parts of their whole having the piss taken out of them, and it's important to know which those places are.

I remember once doing a phone interview for the *Manchester Evening News* to promote the show. I could hear by the journalist's tone of voice that he didn't like me. He was sarcastic and taking the piss at every opportunity. I thought no more about it, as I don't voraciously follow up every interview I've done to see if it's positive. However, while I was in the hotel bar in Manchester with Jeff and John and a couple of sound guys who were touring with us, one of the sound guys, called Simon, happened to mention that he had seen the interview, although he hadn't read it all. Normally, there were lots of free copies lying around in this particular hotel, but I couldn't see a single one. So I went to the desk and asked if I could borrow one. The concierge handed his over and I grew increasingly depressed as I read a complete demolition of my character. Apparently I was vain, full of false modesty, not funny but boring . . . and so it went on. Our planned night out clubbing was replaced by me hiding in my room with a bottle of vodka, getting rat-arsed and refusing to talk to anyone.

Yes, I know – self-pitying and childish . . . I just am sometimes. Poor Simon the sound man felt very guilty. What had actually happened was that Jeff and John had read the interview and, thinking it really unpleasant, had thrown all the free copies of it in the bin while I was in the lav. Not knowing this, poor Simon had mentioned it and led me right down the road to a dose of reality. Still, by the next morning I was over it.

On a separate occasion, in Manchester, John took on an entire rugby team – and came off worse, surprisingly – and I found one of our sound men asleep in the corridor of the hotel when I got up in the morning. Those were the days, my friend.

## Middlesbrough

They don't really laugh in Middlesbrough, but go completely mental at the end of the show. I have checked this out with other comics and they all say the same. Had a first there too. Got a note from some bloke asking me to propose on his behalf. It was accepted by said lady.

I did a student gig there once and was told at the local poly which was about to become a university that the students had requested it be named Central

University (of) Northern Tyneside. Yes, that acronym would certainly have been classy.

Also, Middlesbrough is the place where I have been most off my head following a drinking sesh and foolishly accepting a blue tablet from a bloke I didn't really know.

## Nottingham

I have done Nottingham quite a few times and every time I step out onto the stage and face the audience, they appear to be completely pissed, even on a couple of Sunday nights when I've been there. Also, they seem to be really keen to join in, and a higher than average number of audience members just throw what appear to be random thoughts into the ether. None of it is ever particularly malevolent; they just want to join in.

I once did a gig in Nottingham (I think it was Nottingham, forgive me, it may have been Leicester) next to a roller-skating rink.

Rather foolishly, as we had got there early and had a bit of time to spare, we decided to go roller-skating. I have always been rubbish at that sort of thing, but got stuck in with enthusiasm, and within a minute or so, having fallen several times I found myself plunging towards the floor head first and gave myself a really nasty crack on the skull. I didn't get knocked out, but I did feel quite weird. On top of that, ridiculously I had a few beers and by the time the show was due to start I felt decidedly woozy and out of touch with reality. It may have been concussion, I don't know.

The show was delayed and because it was Nottingham (or Leicester) the audience weren't having it, and after five minutes, set up a chant of 'Why are we waiting?' – the only time this has ever happened to me. As there was no back-stage area because of the way the stage had been constructed, I had to go on stage to introduce Andy – and given that I was a bit bonkers, I lambasted the audience in a far more aggressive way than I would do normally. It didn't set the scene for a very friendly night and poor old Andy had to go on after this and try to rein things in. We got through it, but it was perhaps the strangest mental state I've ever been in when faced with a performance.

### Oxford

I was slightly on edge in Oxford one night, having received a weird letter the night before in Winchester, which made no sense whatsoever, apart from numerous, rather unsettling mentions of Peter Sutcliffe. Off the Kerb kindly provided a big scary guy called Tony, should the letter-writer turn up and try to do damage. Thankfully he didn't.

**Sevenoaks**

Sevenoaks should really be renamed Oneoaks, having lost six of its famous oaks in the great storm of 1987. I have worked there a number of times. On one occasion, Andy was completely stuck on the M40 in one of those traffic jams that just doesn't move for hours. Eventually, it seemed he wasn't going to get there (thank the Lord for mobile phones – at least I knew he wasn't splatted against a tree), so I had to do the whole show on my own.

You might have guessed that I'm not one of those comics that has hours and hours of spare material, so I had to quickly sit down with a pen and paper and drag up some old material from the recesses of my rather badly functioning memory. Success on these occasions also depends on whether the audience will play ball, because one way of stretching things out is to muck about with them. If they sit there in silence staring at you as if you are a disturbed impostor, this doesn't really work, but thankfully the God of Comedy was on my side and I managed to do two forty-five-minute sets which they seemed perfectly satisfied with.

On another occasion I arrived at the same theatre in Sevenoaks to discover that owing to popular demand, forty extra tickets had been sold and the excess punters had been accommodated *on the stage*.

So I found myself performing, placed between four rows of audience, the ones toward the back having a panoramic view of my arse. It wasn't ideal (for them, I would have thought) but again, having to deal with pretty much any eventuality, the solution seemed to be relentlessly taking the piss out of the poor sods who'd had the misfortune to be placed on the stage.

## Warrington

I've been to Warrington a few times and they are well lary there in a fun way, especially the women. One night after a very, very lively (for 'lively', read 'very pissed') gig, as we left by the stage door, Andy the support act was pursued the few yards to the car by a posse of big scary women shouting, 'Show us yer helmet!' I've never seen him looking so terrified. Made me laugh, though.

## Wolverhampton

Wolverhampton is one of those places that people take the piss out of, for it being a bit shit. Granted, it's not the most attractive place in the universe, but I have a real fondness for it. One night, doing the Wulfrun Hall, there was a fire alarm right in the middle of my set. We all duly filed out to the side of the building, where I did my best to carry on, bawling at the top of my voice, but it wasn't terribly successful, and eventually, we were all let back in and carried on as normal.

# Tour Diary

You might be wondering how I remember all this stuff and it's a good question to ask. I have the memory of a pissed goldfish and therefore in my head it is the spectacular moments of my life that tend to stick in the memory banks.

I have, however, kept diaries, but they are not the well-written, lovingly cared for, intelligible and insightful tomes that certain people have managed. No, I'm afraid they're a motley collection of books, notepads and random scraps of paper, written when I was bored, depressed or slightly bonkers. Consequently, you might assume they are a bit rubbish and indeed you'd be right – a lot of them are. But occasionally I come across bits which are quite interesting, not in a *QI*, Stephen Fry sense, but hopefully they add to the whole.

The following is the account of a short tour, spread out over three or four weeks so I could get back home every night.

*Northampton*
Bloody awful headache made worse by one or two drunken people shouting nonsense at me. Reasonable gig in the circs. My friend Mel from college days turned up with some friends. Had a drink after and slunk gratefully into the car.

*Aberystwyth*
Aberystwyth is bloody miles away. They seemed pleased to see us.

*York*
They loved all local paper stuff. Lots of joining in.

*Portsmouth*
Terrible traffic, got there late, very rushed, put make-up on like a five year old.

*Grimsby*
Grim by name . . .

*Dartford*
Felt pleased could bring some joy to Dartford.

*Barnstaple*
Last time I did a gig here, I cried. Not so this time. Warm and fairly bonkers audience who don't see women comics very often, I get the feeling. They were a bit squeamish about the ruder material.

*Halifax*
They were miserable; me too.

*Oxford*
Dreaming spires? Bloody pissed, more like.

*Derby*
Can't stop thinking the base of the English KKK is near here. None in though, thankfully, I don't think.

*King's Lynn*
Why isn't there a motorway to King's Lynn? Stuck behind lorries, tractors, caravans . . . you name it, they were all on the road. Frazzled and grumpy, but don't think they noticed.

*Liverpool*
Cheeky as ever, ranging from quite drunk to
virtually unconscious. Good gig.

*Hayes*
Hayes is near Uxbridge.

*Hull*
Saw a sheet attached to a house saying, *Happy
30th birthday, Nan.*

*Bradford*
I love Bradford.

*Yeovil*
Good sandwiches for a change, rather than the
usual sweaty cheese. Local paper very sweet –
all dog poo and teenagers.

*Newtown*
Why don't people like the Welsh? I bloody love
'em.

# Writing and Doing the Joke Thing

Oh Gawd, where do I start? Producing stand-up material is such a strange mercurial thing that it's hard to pin down. Besides, there are so many different types of stand-up that it's difficult to categorise them. You have, for example, stream of consciousness stand-up, the sort Eddie Izzard does brilliantly, which I have always thought was similar to the symptoms in individuals who suffer from bi-polar disorder and who are in the manic phase of their illness.

This is because when people are in the manic phase, they have something called 'pressure of speech' and 'flight of ideas' which means they splurge out the first thing that comes into their head, and the rate of their speech is so fast and difficult to follow that it can appear like a surreal comedy routine. I remember a manic patient who was a quite delightful posh bloke who had been ill on and off for years, being admitted under a section of the Mental Health Act, which meant he was detained against his will as he was a danger to himself or others. An hour or so after he got there, he came up to the hatch where we were serving up lunch . . .

His speech went something like this:

*Him*: 'Splat that on, darling, splat it on, splat it on, come on, come on . . . and I'll have a spoonful of those little green fuckers [peas] yes, yes, yes, more green fuckers than that, more green fuckers, crikey you're fat, been eating your green fuckers, have you? You're a big girl, you're a very big girl . . . give me some of those little bastards too, will you, the yellow bastards, come on, the yellow bastards [sweetcorn]. Come on, custard as well . . .'

*Me:* 'But you normally have custard with pudding.'

*Him:* 'Not me, love, I have it all on together, pour

77

it on.' STARTS SINGING: 'Pour the fucker on, pour the fucker on . . . ee-i-addio, for fuck's sake pour it on.'

*Me:* 'I can't, it'll taste horrible.'

*Him:* 'Don't care, darling, don't give a flying fuck . . .' AT THIS POINT, HE POURS CUSTARD ON HIS HEAD AND STARTS TO DANCE, SINGING TO THE TUNE OF 'KNEES UP MOTHER BROWN':

'Custard on me head, custard on me head . . .'

We nurses then distract him and someone takes him off to get cleaned up.

I'm not attempting an exhaustive investigation of types of jokes here, but a slightly more scattergun analysis of the sort of jokes I do.

Most comics do the traditional form of stand-up which involves a build-up to the joke and then the punch line, which is usually a reveal or something unexpected.

For example, an early line I did was, 'I'm anorexic,' (hopefully people laugh at this point because I'm obviously not), and then I follow it up with, 'because anorexic people look in the mirror and think they look fat, and so do I.'

Anorexics thinking they look fat has to be a well-known symptom of the illness or else the audience won't get the joke. I have had some complaints from people who are relatives of anorexics, but I'm not having a go at anorexics, I'm having a go at myself.

## Comedy Poems

On occasion I have written comedy poems. When I'm writing them I always think it's important to combine two genres, so the clash between them adds even more humour.

For example, a few years ago I was asked to perform 'something different' at a benefit that I would never normally do, so I wrote an ode to the menopause which was based on Shakespeare.

It went like this:

### ODE TO THE CHANGE

But hark! What light through yonder window breaks?
Oh no, a day that heralds wing-ed towel,

# Jo Brand

Transforming me into a vicious hag,
With all the bonhomie of Mr Simon Cowell.

Oh will this hellish torment never end?
When will my meno ever pause?
All I want for Christmas is a
Day off periods, please Santa Claus.

Hurry, menopause, and take me over,
I don't care any more, just do your work,
So my ovaries ain't gonna go no more,
I couldn't give a flying furk.

Strange symptoms I am told must be expected,
I will embrace them, love them, use them well
As surfing on the gushes and the flushes,
I bulk-buy gin and slap on KY® jell.

For the quality of mucus is not strained, it dries,
    hair falls,
And ends up on your chin,
And when you saunter to your local pub,
They shout, 'Hooray! Brian Blessed's in.'

If HRT's the lubricant of love,

I will transform into a stoutish Barbie,
Although my beloved may well say,
That I remind him more of Mr R. Mugabe.

Then I'll sit in bed all day and call for chocolate,
Hurrah, I hear the sound of husband's door key
Now is the winter of my discontent,
Made glorious summer by this bar of Yorkie.

This was performed at a benefit show at the National Theatre and the audience weren't particularly impressed by my idiot's guide to Shakespeare.

And here's another poem I performed for a bit after Princess Anne's son Peter married a Canadian called Autumn Kelly. It's called:

## THE FALL OF THE HOUSE OF WINDSOR

Marry me, Autumn Kelly, we'll have a massive party and
    get pissed.
I'd love to, but you silly sod, you're not on the Civil
    List.
We can't afford a lavish do, we haven't got a bean,
Oh fuck it then, let's flog the pics to *Hello!* magazine.

We'll get your nan there, Pete, with her crown on,
    what a lark.
And your granddad will, I'm sure, spew out the odd
    racist remark.
And your Uncle Charlie will be running round, all prissy
    and manic,
Sniffing at the vol au vents in case they're not organic.

And security will lurk about, behaving like the Stasi,
And perhaps your cousin Harry will dress up as a Nazi.
And giggling debs and vacuous chinless wonders will
    abound,
As the great ship of the monarchy begins to run
    aground.
And will our grasping and our greed not be seen as a
    bad thing?
No, the public will just love it, they'll all admire your
    bling.
We sip champagne all night and raise two fingers to the
    twats,
They're as bloody daft as one of Cousin Beatrice's hats.

But it might have the same effect as *It's A Royal
    Knockout*.
We could risk opprobrium and a palace lock-out.

The older royals might treat us like we've got the lurgy,
Fear not, my sweet, that's an honour just reserved for
  Fergie.

## Puns
Puns tend to be the stock in trade of the traditional comedian, although occasionally I'll bung a few in. Here's one:

  'My ex-boyfriend came round last week – which was weird 'cause I didn't even know he was in a coma.'

## Pure Abuse
If I want to have a go at people I don't like, the abuse just needs to be comedied up a bit and delivered with enough conviction. Add a bit of alliteration and you will find that even a phrase like 'Toffee-nosed, tedious Tory twat' will get a laugh – although not a very big one, obviously.

## Funny Stories
Quite a few things that have happened to me make me laugh, so occasionally I will take the risk that they will make the audience laugh too. For example, a few years ago I received some strange fan letters from a guy who also sent me several pictures of himself.

They were somewhat unsettling. Then one night, I was watching a documentary about stalkers and there he was on screen, stalking a woman in Essex. All I had to add was, 'Two-timing bastard!' to make a joke.

## Heckle Put-downs

Prepared heckle put-downs should be jokes in themselves and should be really funny i.e. funnier than the original heckle if you're going to take the hecklers on. Just thinking about what sort of heckles I might get enabled me to write appropriate jokes for a series of possibilities e.g. 'Where's your girlfriend? Outside grazing, I presume.'

## Irony

Irony is a great staple of the British comic and identifiable on the continent of America even though we're always saying it isn't. Everyone gets it, so it enables me to do jokes like moving the microphone out of the way at the beginning of my set and saying, 'I'm just going to move this, or you won't be able to see me otherwise.'

## Shock Jokes

Shocking jokes get journalists in the right-wing tabloids very hot under the collar. The proponents of these sort of jokes these days are Frankie Boyle and Jimmy Carr, and they shock because they have a go at groups who have made it clear they don't think it's on to take the piss out of them – such as people with a disability. I always tried to turn this round and point my joke gun at white men, the most powerful group in our society, thus: 'I think they should change the law and allow women to be armed. Then we would be safer in public. We could shoot anyone at night that threatened us, and in fact any bloke that got on our nerves.'

This 'misfired' and didn't go down too well with the unreconstructed males in the audience, as I'm sure you can imagine.

I think the joke I've done that most shocked people, judging by their reaction anyway, was a joke about the Jennifer (daughter of David) Lynch film *Boxing Helena*. I never saw the film but the plot, very simply put, involves a surgeon amputating a woman's arms and legs and keeping her in a box.

I explained this premise to the audience, who received the information very matter-of-factly, and then I said I was worried about how such a woman would cope with personal hygiene without any arms or legs. I went on to ask them to imagine what it would be like for her having periods, trapped as she was like this in a box, and particularly if it was a cardboard box, how it would get all soggy and revolting. At this point there would be, without fail, a noise from the audience which signified their revulsion at the mention of periods and sogginess. I would then say, 'Oh I see, you were quite happy with the idea of a woman having her arms and legs chopped off and being put in a box, but you seem to be completely revolted by the idea of her having a period. What's the matter with you?'

Some of the audience would laugh and applaud; others would just continue to be revolted. I was trying to make a point about how ridiculous some of our taboos are. Even in this day and age it seems so pathetic to me that we have to shroud periods in ridiculously euphemistic terms, but we are quite happy to see women being mutilated for our entertainment. Funny old world, ain't it?

As far as actually thinking of and writing the jokes, it's hard to put my finger on how I actually do it. I very rarely sit down at my computer and write for hours on end, because I simply don't have the time (or the inclination) to do this. I always have hundreds of half-filled little notebooks everywhere with scribbled ideas for jokes, or stuff I have read in the paper that I think would make a good routine. Jokes tend to ferment in my head over a few days rather than present themselves on the page fully formed.

Sometimes, I'll wake up in the middle of the night with the most brilliant joke in the history of the universe in my head and then go straight back to sleep having failed to write it down. When I wake up in the morning, of course the bloody thing has flown out of my brain, never to return. Sometimes I can't find a pen so I'll write on my hand with eyeliner or lipstick, and many's the occasion when I discover a scrap of paper with a smudged bit of lipstick on it and wonder wistfully if that would have won the Joke of the Year competition.

With me, my jokes tend to be highly structured. They certainly were when I started. Every single word in my set was pored over, learned by heart and parroted at an audience in a pretty predictable way. That's why, when I first started, my voice sounded so stupid and flat. As I got more relaxed, so did my voice and I was able to loosen up and not be so obsessive about learning everything parrot-fashion.

These days it's difficult to do new stuff. Audiences have a certain expectation of you, so if you do ten minutes of new material that bombs, they understandably feel a bit short-changed and rightly so. Comics approach new stuff in different ways. Some hide in tiny little theatres in the middle of nowhere and punt out an hour of new stuff to a small audience who may just be pleased they are there. Others disguise bits of new stand-up in their current routine, which is what I tend to do. This means that sometimes I hang on to ancient material for too long, but I am too much of a cowardy custard to replace it all in one fell swoop with a potentially rubbish new set.

I also write with my friend Mark Kelly from time to time because my life got to the stage where it was so busy that if I had a benefit coming up or telly that I needed jokes for, I simply didn't have the time to do it all myself. Mark, who is also a comic on the circuit, writes some excellent lines for me. We have a similar hit rate. One in ten ideas seem to work but I am very grateful to him for coming up with brilliant one-liners like this:

'My husband never learned to drive . . . in my opinion.'

## Making It to the Top

There are many great comics who should be house-hold names yet who remain in the shallows of comedy renown. The fame achieved by some people in the world of comedy is not really about how good a comic they are, it is more about a combination of several things. The most important of these are:

## 1. Luck

Being in the right place at the right time and representing what the important people in television perceive to be the comedy zeitgeist. Let's take Russell Brand as an example. Although Russell is a good comic, stand-up is not his forte. Russell happened to grab people's attention, when he was on the show that followed *Big Brother* – *Big Brother's Big Mouth* – in which I think he was genius. He is very good at responding on his feet, he has huge charm and his use of slightly Victorian, literary language just happened to sit well in this particular show, because he was impudent, imaginative and quick. Added to this, he was perfect tabloid fodder, being the contemporary equivalent of Beau Brummell, a mercurial ladies' man, who seemed somewhat other-worldly, like a modern-day Oscar Wilde. And so it was this platform from which he was launched into the firmament, rather than the platform of his stand-up.

America has grasped him to her bosom. That's because America seems to love a British fop and Russell is that irresistible combination of a highly intelligent, ordinary, working-class guy who has a foot in both camps. It's a shame to me that he has been tempted to appear in films that I can't even be bothered to see because they sound so middle-of-the-road. The same goes for Ricky Gervais. Why has he gone to America? Why has the subtlety of his dark, malevolent wit been shovelled into the gaping, uncompromising, populist maw of the Hollywood machine, which can only result in a watering-down of his strength? Is it money? Is it global fame? I don't know. Am I just envious? I can honestly say I'm not – and so maybe the problem is mine, in that case!

## 2. Talent

I have put talent second because I believe it is less important than luck. The list of neglected comedy talent is stuffed with extremely funny, potentially huge comedians: Johnny Immaterial (Jonathan Meres) John Hegley, Boothby Graffoe (James Martyn Rogers), Hattie Hayridge, Linda Smith (God rest her lovely comedy soul, even though she didn't believe in Him), and many others who seem to have missed their opportunity as it passed silently by them.

3. Television execs
Those powerful people in television, who get to point to a comic as if they are laid on a table like a buffet, play a huge part in who makes it and who doesn't. And if they don't like you, you're going to struggle, unless you're so popular, they cannot ignore you.

4. Not being like another comic
No aspiring comic should base their act on someone they admire. Individuality of thought and performance is what TV people are looking for, and if you model yourself on, say, Jack Dee or Billy Connolly, it's obvious that if those people have already become household names, a wishy-washy version of them, which you will invariably seem, is not what's required.

# Tip-Top Comedy Moments

I have narrowed down my favourite comedy moments to half a dozen, leaving out an incident in a hotel with two comics which I am sworn not to repeat.

One of my all-time favourite comedies is *Fawlty Towers*. Despite the race and gender stereotypes, which have been retrospectively condemned by many, there is so much to admire about this series. Basil Fawlty is a supreme comedy character, and there are some sublime moments. We all have our favourites, but one of mine is the scene when the grumpy old guest complains about the view, and Basil launches into a rant about what she'd expected: 'Hordes of wildebeest sweeping majestically across the plain,' for example.

Just recently, I stayed in a very upmarket hotel en route from Cornwall. I had performed at a lovely small theatre near Liskeard and was travelling to a village near Hastings where I was opening my brother's fete, because ex-*Doctor Who* Tom Baker had pulled out at the last minute. (Probably too many Cybermen encroaching on Winchelsea.)

At the hotel, a very sweet young man took me to my room and showed me where everything was, and he commented particularly on the wonderful view before drawing back the curtains to show me. Unfortunately, he had forgotten it was midnight and there wasn't a bleeding view, but it was very entertaining nevertheless.

Dawn French and Jennifer Saunders gave me another top comedy moment when they came up with their pervy, fat old geezers who would attempt to shag anything (and it didn't even have to move) including the side of an armchair. I remember first seeing them and laughing till I cried. Every detail was so accurate, right down to the fact that so many men of that ilk seem to think that women are 'gagging for it' and they are the blokes to give it to them. Sublime.

*Monty Python* was woven into the fabric of my teenage years, and most of the sketches I loved featured Terry

Jones dressed up as a woman. There was something about the floral fifties' dress and wrinkly stockings on his skinny legs that was hysterical, and in *The Meaning of Life*, as a pregnant mother plopping out babies at the sink while washing up. I laughed every time I thought of it, even slightly inappropriately in public from time to time.

*Airplane* is one of my all-time favourite comedy films, because it is so silly and has so many gems of funniness in it. I think my favourite character was the one played by Lloyd Bridges who works in the airport and is a typically stressed and out-of-control man. Throughout the film we return to him time and time again, as he says the immortal lines, 'I picked the wrong week to give up smoking/drinking/amphetamines/glue-sniffing' and sinks back into a mire of substance abuse. As an oral person who has the potential to be addicted to all these things, it was my perfect kind of comedy.

Richard Pryor was a comedy genius, and to some extent many of the comedy acts that followed him drew upon his brilliant evocations of ordinary life as a black working-class person in America (even though a lot of the comics were neither black nor lived in America). No one could possibly fail to laugh at his anthropomorphising of his pets and how they fitted into the family hierarchy.

*Only Fools and Horses* is another comedy that is full of stereotypes, and although I love the supreme timing of Del Boy's fall backwards through the bar after the barman has unwittingly left a gap there, my favourite episode involves the crash to the floor of the priceless chandelier, because Grandad has loosened the wrong one while Del Boy and Rodney wait haplessly beneath another one with a sheet.

And that – as they say in the biz – is your lot, folks.

# On Tour (or In a Plane for Hours)

Doing stand-up abroad is a bit weird given that in some countries the cultural gap is so enormous that the audience is completely puzzled by your jokes. Of course, the major barrier is language, which means that British comics are confined to those countries that speak English as a first language or fluently as a second language.

Therefore the main countries available to us are America, Canada, Australia and a vast selection of other countries in which ex-pats live such as Dubai and Hong Kong.

My limited experience includes only Canada, Australia, and parts of Europe such as Germany and Holland, where you will find that the natives speak better English than we do most of the time. (I exclude Australia from that statement.)

## Canada

I have been to Canada twice, both times for the Montreal Comedy Festival, which has intimate connections with Edinburgh and the big comedy agencies over here. Every year, a scout from Montreal will come over to England to watch comedy and then invite various comics to go over and perform at their festival. At the time I went, there was a comedy programme linked to it which was shown on Channel Four, called *Just for Laughs*.

I was invited following an Edinburgh performance and despite my dislike of flying I decided to grit my teeth and go for it. Rumour had it that some of the big American agents wandered around Montreal, which was obviously easier for them to travel to, rather than coming to England, and you might get yourself an HBO (Home Box Office – big comedy channel) special or something even better.

I didn't really want to go to America and work, but

decided it would do no harm to my career if I at least showed up. So I found myself queuing at Heathrow, somewhat anxious about the nine-hour flight but determined to mitigate the nerves with a bout of extreme smoking. (There is more about smoking later; it gets its very own chapter. See *A Nasty Habit*, page 244).

This was in the early nineties, and at that point everyone was still smoking their heads off on planes, so as I reached the desk with my friend Sue, I confidently requested a smoking seat up the back, just like being at the back of the school bus.

The woman on the desk – sneeringly, I thought – informed me that it was a No Smoking flight and at that instant I hated her more than I have ever hated anyone. In the few seconds I had, the idea ran through my head that I might just as well go home and forget the whole bloody thing. However, I reasoned I had got this far, and decided to batten down the emotional hatches and go for it.

It wasn't a pleasant experience; there was a fair bit of turbulence and I arrived at the other end feeling jaded and thrown about. Montreal seemed like a slightly smaller, nicer version of America with its glass towers gleaming in the sun, the centrepiece being a huge pink tower which was immediately named by one wag 'The Jolly Pink Penis'. On the flight with me were Frank Skinner, Jerry Sadowitz and Craig Charles . . . all ready to fire a handful of jokes at the Canadians and see if they laughed.

We were put up in what I considered, with my limited experience, to be a very flash hotel and immediately set to what comics are famous for – a lot of drinking.

In order to crank ourselves up for the Comedy Gala (in Canada it is pronounced 'Gayla') we had the opportunity to try out our material in smaller clubs to see if it worked. I found myself in one show called *The Nasty Show* (in Canada pronounced 'Nair-sty') and it couldn't have been more apt, making me seem very mild. It displayed the talents of some most unpalatable racist, misogynist comedians, and when one of them vomited out a really horrible joke about Oprah Winfrey, I began to wonder if I was in the right place.

That night, pissed and fuelled by righteous indignation, I picked up my phone about two o'clock in the morning and called the room of the comic in question to protest about his material. I'm afraid I only managed the two words, 'You're shit,' and then put the phone down. Yes, not exactly a well-reasoned academic argument, I know, and much as I'd like to apologise for my appalling behaviour, I'm not going to. He was a deeply unsavoury man and I hope Oprah appreciates all my efforts on her behalf. I do realise I could have been more grown up about it, but I'm not very grown up when I've had a few – or when I haven't.

Incidentally, my material wasn't going down all that well either. It was around the time of the Gulf War and I was doing some stuff about Saddam Hussein. When the audience looked blankly at me as if to say, 'Who the hell is Saddam Hussein?' I gave up and went back to the fat jokes, which they seemed to like.

During this trip we attempted to do some sociable things to get to know our surroundings, and apparently one of the must-dos was a trip on the rapids. We all arrived down at the riverside one morning and were kitted out in life-jackets and shepherded onto a big boat which seated about thirty people. There then ensued what seemed like a combination of being shaken about so much that your bones rattled whilst continuously having buckets of water thrown over you. It was good fun. However, it was too much for one of our party who, fuelled by extreme anxiety, went into a sort of catatonic state of paralysis. A little boat bustled over to our bigger boat and he was taken off, poor sod, as stiff as a board.

I came up against a few unlikeable comedians on

that trip. Each Montreal Festival flies in an elderly statesman of comedy, and for my first trip there it was Milton Berle. To be honest, I'd never heard of him, but people assured me he was dead famous in the States. Also, as I am not at the nerdy end of the comedy world, I haven't assiduously studied the lives of all comics going back to the Ice Age which certainly some of my peer group have done. Milton Berle looked about 150 but he may only have been in his eighties. He was to compere the Gala show I was doing. This involved bursting out of a big box at the back of the stage, and as it's not something we all do every day, we had to go to the 3,200-seater theatre to rehearse it in case we walked out of the box backwards, I suppose, or accidentally burst out of the side.

We were all introduced to Milton Berle at this point and his interpersonal skills with women seemed to be somewhat lacking. As someone gestured at me and said, 'And this is Jo Brand,' he moved towards me, saying, 'Well, come here then, girl, I'm not going to touch your titties.'

First of all, I hate that word 'titties' – it's a word children and pervy old men use – and he obviously fell into the latter category. I was in another country, faced with a very famous American comic, and tongue-tied for those reasons. I regret not giving the old fart as good as I got.

The night of the Gala arrived and terrifying it was too. I had never performed in front of such a big audience before and was nervous as hell. However, I managed to come out of the front of the box and deliver my words all in the right order, to some nice laughs and applause.

Unfortunately, Jerry Sadowitz didn't fare quite so well. This may be to do with the fact that he opened his set by saying, 'Good evening, moose fuckers.' I'm not sure the Canadians were particularly enamoured with that title, since a man right at the back got out of his seat, strolled nonchalantly down the steps, got up on stage and lamped Jerry right in the face. Jerry got up and was hit again before a security man ambled across the stage and removed the offender in as congratulatory a way as he could possibly have managed. It was the talk of the festival, of course, and most of us felt relieved that it wasn't us.

I was on my way to the after-show party when an audience member cornered me in the corridor.

'Well done,' he enthused, 'and I thought it was particularly funny that you have two balloons down your front.

They looked so natural.' Well, I didn't have any balloons down my front and, worried he was going to do a Milton Berle and check, I legged it.

After we'd had a few drinks, we went for a meal at a restaurant nearby where lots of the comics and agents hung out. As I was heading back from the toilet to join my friends, I passed a table that appeared to be populated by the Italian Mafia: lots of guys in sharp suits doing the wearing-sunglasses-inside thing. No women. As I passed, one of them stared straight at me. Well, I think he was looking at me; his face was turned in my direction. He initially pointed at me without a word and then curled his finger in a supercilious, beckoning motion.

Maybe he thinks I'm a waitress, I thought, but instead of politely informing him I wasn't, and fuelled by a couple of sherries, I looked at him and said, 'Piss off, you twat.'

On arrival back at my table I asked a Canadian comic who the group of Mafia lookey-likeys were that had attempted to detain me.

'Oh, they're all really important American agents,' he replied.

Goodbye, Hollywood.

## Montreal 2

Weirdly, I can't recall much about my second Montreal trip. I took my friend Waggly with me that time and it is only a very stressful epic journey I remember – a trip to the Niagara Falls, which I decided I really wanted to see in person, as it were.

We intended to hire a car and drive there and back in a day on my day off: We had failed to take into account a few very important things. Firstly, we didn't really know where the fuck we were going, secondly I'd never driven an automatic car on the wrong side of the road, and thirdly it was roughly a 900-mile round trip.

Getting out of Montreal itself was like some sort of nightmare odyssey. I made several wrong turns, entries down one-way streets and at one point we ended up on what appeared to be a massive building site. A bloke in a fluorescent jacket approached and I thought with some relief that he was going to redirect us. So I wound down the window to apologise and ask directions. His words: 'Move, bitch.' I did.

After roughly six hours of driving we neared our destination. The Niagara Falls is set in a big park and we could hear the roar of the water as we entered.

'Look,' cried Waggly, all excited. 'There it is!'

'It' turned out to be a fountain, and after some gentle piss-taking from me, we parked opposite the great whooshing waterfall itself. Unfortunately, by this time it was getting dark and I was already worried about how long it was going to take us to get back. So we must have done the quickest surveillance of the Falls anyone has ever done, before we got back in the car and drove for another six/seven hours, arriving back in Montreal exhausted and very slightly tearful.

Waggly and I had a lovely time in Montreal, mainly staying in bed very late, mooching round town admiring the architecture, sitting in cafés doing bog-all for hours on end, and recovering from our odyssey to Niagara Falls. Waggly was the perfect companion, happy to go with the flow, pleased to be there, endlessly entertaining and cheerful.

One evening when I had a night off we trawled the bars and clubs together, getting more pissed as we went. We ended up in a sort of wine bar-type place and sat down at a table and ordered a bottle of wine. Two guys moved in and started trying to chat us up. This was most unusual for me, not so much for Waggly who is lovely-looking and slim. But as a fat person you soon learn that your role is to be that of the quirky, joke-cracking friend and that you are going to get the flawed friend or God forbid what they call 'a chubby chaser', and down that road lie untold horrors for me. Even to this day, I so resent being judged by my appearance on first meeting, that it makes my blood boil when on-sight assessments are made of me and I cannot help but turn into a piss-taking, offhand old harridan.

One of the blokes was a reasonably attractive tall thin thing, and the friend was OK, but not in the slightest my cup of tea as he appeared to be slightly to the right of Mussolini and was steadfastly making cracks about Native Americans for our entertainment. Waggly was missing all this as she was engaged in flirty banter with the mate who, for some reason, was not a psycho and maybe was doing his bit for the community by accompanying his friend round.

Pissed as I was, I knew I had to get out of there before I either tipped my drink down the Canadian fascist's front or worse. This is a constant dilemma for friends, I think, when one of them has met someone they're quite keen on and their mate has just met the social equivalent of Jack the Ripper. Given that we were thousands of miles from home, I didn't really want to leave Waggly on her own with her one, as for all I knew they were a double act of perviness hoovering up naive foreign ladies to lock in their cellar. I could not find the opportunity to have a word in Waggly's ear without being heard, so I had to think fast. I decided fainting was probably the best thing to do, and then once we got outside I could give her the option of going back if she really wanted to.

So faint I did. Usually when you faint, your body goes floppy so you sink to the ground and tend not to get injured. This was not the case with me. So worried was I about it looking convincing that I stood up first and said something like, 'I don't feel well,' and then did my best to plunge to the ground in true drama-school-end-of-term-play fashion. On the way down I hit my head on the side of the marble table and nearly went, 'Fuck, that *hurt*,' but managed to stop myself. Waggly panicked slightly whilst I, with my instant migraine, attempted not to laugh.

I reckon I did a pretty good impression of coming round in a woozy fashion and Waggly helped me up and took me outside for some fresh air, promising Mr Chatter Upper she'd be back in a minute. Mr Pervo looked completely disinterested and out of one slightly open eye I noticed him scanning the bar for fresh stoutness.

Waggly supported me outside, and as soon as we were out of earshot I told her that my 'partner' was a complete tosspot and I had to escape. I immediately apologised to her and said I knew she liked hers and if she really wanted to stay she could, but I felt worried about leaving her. Her reply, 'What are you talking about? He's a complete wanker – I was only staying because I thought you wanted to.' Oh how we laughed, oh how we legged it, oh how we didn't look back.

If our 'friends' are reading this, I apologise for our unannounced exit and I hope you are both happily married with patient wives (one quite fat) and lovely children. To be perfectly honest and no offence to the people of Canada, but it just wasn't in my plans to marry a Canadian chubby chaser.

**Australia**

I toured Australia in the early nineties and found it strange travelling to the other side of the world and staying there for six weeks. I am not a natural traveller as I tend to prefer journeys in my head which are so much easier, and I missed home, friends and family hugely.

We were lucky that the Australian tour company paid for a first-class air ticket for myself, my friend and support act, Jeff Green, and John, our tour manager. We didn't have to sit squashed for hours in tiny seats shoulder to shoulder with each other but could stretch out, watch a film and see ourselves fly over the edge of the world as the sun came up.

I had known Jeff for a long time and we were good friends. He is from Chester and has a cheekiness that is associated with nearby Liverpool. His material is great; it has a familiarity to it and an easy rhythm, as well as being enormously funny. Jeff is a prime example of someone who, in my opinion, should most definitely be a household name by now.

Right, back to Australia. I was slightly surprised when we landed and someone got on the plane and processed down the aisle spraying us with some sort of disinfectant as if we were lepers.

Our first port of call was Sydney, said to be one of the more sophisticated of the Australian cities. We were bunged in a very nice hotel and had a couple of days to chill out before the first gig. The time of year was May, so I suppose we were heading towards their winter, but it felt pretty damn warm to me.

To some extent, once you are in a city, there is not a huge amount of difference where you are in the world. Hotel rooms all look the same and you find the same products, especially the posh ones, pretty much wherever you are. Likewise, again to some extent, the audiences.

I did quite a bit of telly to promote the tour. Firstly, a talent show with a very camp American comic, Scott Capurro. Between us we agreed that for a laugh we would give really shit marks. Anyway, the first act up was a very cute little girl who sang a very cute song and did a very cute dance. Scott went first on the judging panel and gave her one out of ten. There was uproar and it looked like he might be lynched. They moved on to me and I declared, 'Ten out of ten . . . she's so cute.' Well, I was nearly hoisted onto their shoulders and cheered to the rafters. I don't think Scott was too happy with me for a bit though.

I'm sorry if I upset Scott, because he is very likeable and good fun. He is also extremely filthy and has an ability to make people in audiences do sharp intakes of breath every few seconds or so.

Recently, my friend Betty's seventeen-year-old son went to see him with a mate, and the fools sat in the front row, which I would never advise – especially if you're seeing Scott or Julian Clary – because you will get the piss ripped out of you. The friend had to endure an elongated assault on his appearance and I think it taught him to sit well back in the future.

I was a bit apprehensive about the first gig. Would the audience understand the references, the Bernard

Manning joke about racism, concerns like that? I needn't have worried. The audiences were keen, warm and appreciative.

After Sydney we proceeded to Melbourne: warm, friendly and very laughy gigs, which we all enjoyed. I did notice though that, much to my surprise, there was quite a bit of racism knocking about, particularly amongst younger people. I suppose I just expect older people to be racist in that rather naive way that they have. But to hear a Goth girl who looked like a radical leftie say, 'Fucking Pakis, they get on my nerves,' was a bit of a shock, particularly as the peer group around her didn't bat an eyelid.

We had a little break in proceedings before we went to Perth, our final destination, so I decided, dragging my co-conspirators along, to go to Tasmania to visit a friend and ex-flatmate of mine, Gabe, who was by now a GP with his wife, also a GP, in a small town in the north; as a sideline, he had a deer farm. When we arrived, it was pissing with rain. We spent a very enjoyable, if soaking, night hunting for platypuses, not spotting a single one.

We flew back to Sydney and from there went on to Perth, which is isolated – and feels it – right out on the west coast. The gigs there were great, with cheery, enthusiastic audiences.

After that, even though really we had done bugger-all, we felt like a holiday, so we hired a boat with a man who knew what to do with it and toured the Whitsunday Islands up in the North-East for ten days. The heat was tropical and my ankles turned into foot-balls which wasn't terribly attractive, but we had a good laugh even though John, our tour manager, kept us awake most nights with his titanic snoring.

I also hadn't realised that toileting was such a palaver on a boat. Don't read this next bit if you're slightly squeamish ... but we didn't know that if someone's just had a poo, it's not a good idea to go in for a swim at the same time. The sight of Jeff swimming through a patch of little plops and the look on his face, gave me one of the best laughs of the holiday. It was idyllic though most of the time, turtles swimming past the boat, snorkelling (us, not the turtles) and admiring the fantastically coloured sea-life in a clear azure sea and lounging on the boat as the sun set ... it was pretty much perfect.

**Holland**
The great thing about the Dutch is they speak really good English and watch lots of BBC programmes. The only problem they had with my set was 'panty-liner'

but they soon got the gist as I did an award-winning mime.

Harry Hill was over there too, and it was to him I recounted my huge sense of disappointment when, at the end of the day, I reached for a well-deserved Toblerone in the fridge in my room, only to find someone had already eaten it and stuffed screwed-up paper back into it to make it look like they hadn't.

Of course, the attraction for a lot of people in Amsterdam is the red-light district. Those people do tend to be of the male variety, though. I found it quite surreal and rather disturbing to wander along a street with women all dressed up in the shop windows trying to entice customers in for a quick one. Added to that I've never been a prodigious dope smoker, so cafés selling every variety of the stuff didn't really attract me, populated as they were with glassy-eyed gigglers. So two days was enough for me.

**The Shetland Islands**
I know that, in theory, the Shetlands aren't a foreign country, but they certainly feel as if they are at the end of the world. Once you arrive at Edinburgh airport you have to change planes and get on something that looks like it worked as a back-up plane in the

First World War. As we queued to get on, I couldn't avoid listening to two blokes chatting. One said to the other, 'You know one of these crashed last week, don't you?' To which the other replied, 'Yes, they've got a terrible safety record.'

That's not really what I want to hear as I'm just about to get on one. The gig in the Shetlands was in a tiny theatre and the audience seemed to be so pleased that we'd made the effort to travel in the Plane of Death that I got the feeling we could have said anything and they would have laughed their hand-knitted little socks off. Jeff and I both had absolute stormers and came away from the show with a warm glow. This soon dissolved when we discovered the next morning that we were locked in by fog and it was too risky to take off. Still, better to wait until the fog clears than to enter a lighthouse without having to climb the stairs . . . No, I don't know what that means either.

## Stavanger, Norway

Stavanger is a pretty little town with quite a lot of oil stuff going on (she said knowledgeably). Consequently there are quite a few English and Americans knocking about. We went on the day after the General Election in 1997, and one of the friends who came with us was still pissed from the night before when we knocked on her door, and sat through the flight in a haze of drunken joy at the thought of Blair getting in. She was in good company though. Shane MacGowan of the Pogues was on our flight looking like my friend was going to feel in about three hours' time. He gave me that weird nod that people on the telly give each other. I suppose it's like a fireman bumping into another fireman.

Customs at Stavanger consisted of a trestle table manned by a bloke in a cap, and as we filed past I noticed that poor Shane was the only one picked out of our bunch and was standing with his suitcase open on the trestle table looking like a naughty ten year old.

I didn't really like the gig. There is something about ex-pat types that makes my hackles rise, although I can't really put my finger on what it is. So I presume I stepped on stage with the wrong attitude and it all went downhill from there until the heckles and general hubbub sent me off slightly earlier than I'd intended.

**Ireland**
Because the Irish speak English, I had assumed that culturally it would be very similar to Britain. That is

definitely not the case. It is indeed a foreign country and they do things differently there.

## Northern Ireland

On my first trip to Northern Ireland, I carried all the preconceptions that most of us do, when all we know about a place is what we've seen on TV or read in the newspapers. The cab driver who took me from the airport to the hotel jokingly told me at the time (early nineties) that quite a few people, mainly businessmen, bob down on the back seat for fear of being picked off by a sniper or a bomb going off. Whether or not it was a figment of my imagination, I certainly found the atmosphere over there to be imbued with an underlying sense of danger, but I am sure that was all self-generated. (Although it is somewhat disconcerting to be told you are staying in 'the most bombed hotel in Belfast'.)

Many people wanted to go and gawp at all the infamous areas of Belfast where the Troubles were focused. I couldn't bring myself to do so, because I felt it was a bit voyeuristic, so I let them get on with it and stayed at the hotel.

My first gig ever in Northern Ireland was at a mainly Protestant university in Belfast, and I wasn't prepared for how pissed and lary they would be. It was like a duel with the audience, and I ended up doing none of my prepared material at all, while they chanted 'Fuck Off You Fat Lesbian!' in unison and seemed to be enjoying themselves enormously. So I pretty much let them get on with it.

I graduated to a bigger theatre in the centre of Belfast some years later, and this was the only occasion on which I've had a piece of clothing thrown at me. About twenty minutes into my set, a pair of light blue, slightly baggy Y-fronts landed on the stage in front of me, having been lobbed from the balcony . . . quite an impressive throw. I picked them up gingerly because I was planning to display them to the audience. They were still warm and a shiver of something went through me and I flung them immediately to the floor. Most unsettling.

I also did a bit of TV in Northern Ireland and appeared on a satirical show which, it turned out, the viewing public there wasn't really ready for. After the episode I appeared on, the series was cancelled – for once nothing to do with me, but down to an impression of Ian Paisley which I think was just too near to the knuckle.

One thing that happens when you do this job is that you tend to meet comedy heroes quite unexpectedly, and it was while a few of us were sitting in the green room watching an old Monty Python episode that the door opened and Michael Palin himself popped his head round.

What a surreal moment! Along with Terry Jones, Michael Palin was always my favourite and I was over-come by that fannish-will-I-say-something-stupid moment and just stared at him as if he was a recently landed alien. He gave us a chirpy 'Hello!' and then disappeared again.

## Republic of Ireland

In the late nineties, I toured the Republic, going from Dublin to Waterford to Cork to Limerick. The audi-ences seemed really shell-shocked by my material and I began to wonder whether I should tone it down a bit. Having done a few gigs before in Ireland at the Kilkenny Festival and a comedy club in Cork, I was quite surprised by the reaction, but it may have been that the theatres I was appearing in had a slightly muffling effect on people's exuberance. Or perhaps they just didn't like me.

During the tour I visited the castle in which the Blarney Stone is situated. Legend has it that if you kiss the Blarney Stone, it will give you the gift of the gab.

However, it's not quite as simple as you think because it is attached rather awkwardly to the castle, and you have to sort of shuffle out on your back looking down over a huge drop. This, and the fact that someone told me that people occasionally piss on the Blarney Stone, rather put me off deciding to snog it.

# Edinburgh: From the Eighties to the Noughties

Edinburgh is comedy Mecca and the city towards which all we comics face in blind obeisance (although blind drunkenness might be a more appropriate metaphor).

It soon becomes apparent that Edinburgh is where it's at if you want to advance your comedy career. The Fringe Festival there gives you the opportunity, which you don't get in London, to showcase your wares. Because there are so many clubs in London, your average producer/TV exec can't be arsed to flog round all the little clubs but prefers to go to Edinburgh for a couple of weeks where all the eager comics are grazing.

Plus, because it is a festival, the execs have the added advantage of many, many reviews – which enables them to weed out the rubbish, so they needn't even bother to go and see the crap shows.

There are hundreds of venues in Edinburgh and hundreds of comics vying for the attention of the public. Bank balances are severely under threat if you are a less experienced comic whose show doesn't sell well; in fact, thousands can be lost by comedians who are either naive or a little too over-confident.

In my day (yes, I know I sound like your grandma, but it was a long time ago), one aimed to appear at one of the top three venues, because they had a guaranteed audience.

The first was the Assembly Rooms – always considered the poshest venue, containing small stages and big ones like the Supper Room. Sounds stuck-up, doesn't it? It was a nice venue and I performed there one year.

Unfortunately, because of the lay-out of the place, you cannot get on to the stage unobserved, to appear, like the Bad Fairy, from back stage, so you have to plop yourself round there before the audience is allowed to enter, fifteen minutes before the show. As nerves are an unwelcome accompaniment of any stand-up show, one needs a wee roughly every ten seconds, and this is just not possible once you have sited yourself behind the curtain. This leaves you with the unwelcome choices of holding on to it, wetting yourself or pissing in a receptacle – boys in lager bottles and girls into something with a wider rim. Sorry to plant this unpleasant image in your minds, but it's a necessity unless you want to appear on stage with a wet patch sullying the front of your attire.

The Assembly Rooms attract the more upmarket, lazier comedy audience who only ever go there and nowhere else, figuring that eventually, every good comic worth their salt will appear there. The Assembly Rooms is presided over by one William Burdett-Coutts. Yes, just as patrician as he sounds, but a softly spoken, quietly humorous individual who I liked immensely, and with whom I never had cause to fall out.

The second of the three best venues, the Pleasance, is exactly what it's called – a pleasant cluster of venues grouped round a central courtyard where people can breeze in and out and watch absent-minded or terrified comics drift through their line of vision on their way to and from shows. On a sunny day, it's lovely to sit at a table with a beer and witness a few impromptu performances of the juggling/street theatre variety. (It has to be said though, that a sunny day in Edinburgh is quite a rare phenomenon.)

The inimitable 'father' of the Pleasance, Christopher Richardson in my day, could often be seen striding round the courtyard, his ample frame clad in an ancient linen suit and straw hat, holding forth about some irritation or other.

The Pleasance had a lovely buzz about it. Studenty, arty, sociable, it was always a pleasure to be at.

The Gilded Balloon can be found in what appears to be a street running underneath the rest of Edinburgh. Epicentre of drunken socialising for most comics, apart from some of the older ones who like a sit-down in the Assembly Rooms, it was the scene of much alcohol- and drug-fuelled shenanigans, and drew a crowd of ne'er-do-wells, both from among the comics and the audience.

I remember once heading towards the place and bumping into Steve Coogan, who informed me that the Pleasance staff had gone on strike and I was to immediately go there and show my solidarity with them. When I said that I'd like to know about the genesis of the dispute, before I made up my mind whether to support them, he said, 'Oh Jo, you're such a liberal.' I think that is the only time I've ever been called a liberal.

The Gilded Balloon was run and managed by one Karen Koren, as feisty a Scotswoman as you could hope to meet. Everyone seemed terrified of her. I thought she was a good laugh. She made sure that the atmosphere of the Gilded Balloon was always slightly edgy and difficult to predict. One way she did this was to put on a late-night show called *Late and Live* which didn't start until after midnight. There was always an interesting combination of mainly English acts and a predominantly Scots audience. The added factor of the late hour also helped to ensure that much heckling of a not entirely complimentary nature went on. My approach was to try and make sure I was as drunk as the audience – which was very, very, very, very, very drunk. I could then respond to them on the level at which they had pitched their alcohol-fuelled comments about my appearance and the content of my material. Also, being this pissed meant the following morning I couldn't remember a bloody thing about how the show had gone which, nine times out of ten, was a blessing.

Having filled you in on the venues I have spent most of my time in, there now follows a brief history of my Edinburgh experiences. It is surprising in some ways that I can remember anything about them at all, given that Edinburgh for me has always been a distant bacchanalian country which is not in any way connected to reality, apart from the wreckage of one's physical and mental state on returning home.

## First Edinburgh, 1988

My first trip to Edinburgh was your standard cabaret show with a compere and two other stand-ups. The compere was Ivor Dembina, a lovable character who I've mentioned before, and with whom I became good friends; at one point we even shared a flat. Ivor ran the comedy venue, the Red Rose in Finsbury Park in North (yuk) London. He was the regular compere there and, like myself, didn't turn over new material at the speed of light like some of the newer, keener comics did. This meant that over the years I came to know his set very well, and jokes of his would be bandied about by most of us in a fond kind of way. Ivor's act was occasionally inconsistent so it has to be said we saw him dying some spectacular deaths on stage from time to time – but that only endeared him more to people.

Ivor was also like your favourite uncle. Bespectacled, sardonic and easygoing, he was always good fun to be with. When we shared a flat, things were pretty amicable between us as for a few months we played 'Who Is The Laziest Flatmate?' We had one huge row once that started over who put a bottle of tomato ketchup away and it escalated into a massive shouting match, but apart from that it was very hard to fall out with Ivor, who had been a teacher before he'd become a comedian, and we rubbed along pretty well together until we moved on.

At an out-of-town club, as compere, Ivor once called the interval and remarked to some guy in the front row, 'All right mate, you start the dancing,' only to discover that the guy in question was 'dancing' because he had a serious physical disability. Much embarrassment ensued, including some audience indignation because they assumed he was taking the piss out of a disabled person.

Also on the bill for my first Edinburgh jaunt were Mark Thomas and James Macabre. Mark Thomas, as I'm sure you will know, is what the London listings magazine *City Limits* used to call a 'polemical' comedian. Fiery, in your face and full of energy, he used to force his way into the consciousness of the audience and held the stage almost as if he was under siege. James Macabre (real name Jim Miller) was altogether different. More understated performance-wise, he was equally powerful as a stand-up. His material was pretty dark and very silly at times, and I think as a trio we were a good balance, each offering a contrast to the others.

We appeared in the Pleasance bar, which was the perfect venue for us as it was the most like the cabaret clubs in London that we were used to, and not theatre-like at all. This did mean that the audience could get quite pissed, as the bar was open all night. Still, we were used to this too, so it suited us.

And get pissed they did.

One of the characteristics of Edinburgh was the unspoken antipathy between the Scots and the English. I say unspoken, but on a number of occasions I was abused for my English accent. However, this was more than made up for by the jocular nature of the vast majority of Scots I met.

My abiding memory of this first Edinburgh was a fight which started at the show. A group of locals, having imbibed a fair bit, got stuck into some heckling during our show. It wasn't particularly nasty, just irritatingly constant, like an itch, and every form of put-down, clever retort, desperate plea that they were ruining the show, went unheard. So we just put our heads down and got through the show as best we could. So far so good.

However, after the show, on our way out to the courtyard to have a well-earned drink, we encountered our
hecklers face to face – two young men and a very lary
woman. She and I began a rather foolish argument
involving a lot of swearing, and at one point, pissed as
she was and probably not really aware of what she was
doing (to give her the benefit of the doubt), the charming
woman stubbed a fag out on my arm. This was more
than I could cope with and, calling for reinforcements,
the argument spilled out into the courtyard and became
a bit of a fight.

Drunken fists were flying. All of us were crap at
fighting, and I suspect to an onlooker it was quite good
comedy. Eventually people were dragged off other
people with the usual clichés of, 'It's not worth it!'
and, 'Leave it out!' and the whole thing was over as
quickly as it had started. It was a baptism of fire for
me as I usually manage to contain myself and get no
further than just verbals.

The other baptism of fire one encounters at
Edinburgh is, of course, reviews. These are hard to
take, unless they're brilliant obviously, which in the
early days for me they often weren't. I convince
myself that if reviews are bad yet constructive and
not personal, that is fair enough. (However, I don't

really believe that.) But it is much worse if they are personal.

In that first year, I remember getting a review that took the piss out of the way I delivered my material in my football-scores style. Unused to this sort of criticism, I saw red. A fantasy developed in my head that when I saw the critic – can't even remember his name now – I would cause him some sort of physical damage. I nursed this fantasy in the evil, black part of my heart until I actually saw the man in question in the Gilded Balloon bar later on in the Festival. By this point, however, the heat had gone out of my anger and I just gave him my hardest stare and moved on.

## Second Edinburgh, 1989

This year I worked at the Gilded Balloon with comics Kevin Day and Michael Redmond. We called the show *Sean Corcoran and Phyllis Holt Present* because I had a character called Phyllis Holt in one of my jokes at the time, and Michael had a character called Sean Corcoran in one of his.

Michael was a lugubrious Irish one-liner merchant whose delivery was slow, measured and expressionless, whereas Kevin Day was your archetypal London cheeky chappie whose jokes always had a sting in the tail and belied his laidback style.

We always performed a little play at the end of the show about Sherlock Holmes, and our main aim was to get as many puns on the phrase 'Elementary, my dear Watson' as we could. Sounds crap? Dear reader, it was, but we loved it. We worked our way through 'A lemon entry', 'alimentary' and many others which mercifully I cannot remember. Weirdly, though, I do remember, word for word, a review we got from a student magazine. No, I don't have a photographic memory. It seared itself into my brain . . .

Because . . .

a) It was short

and

b) It was horrible

The review stated: *Michael Redmond is Irish, Kevin Day is a cheeky Cockney and Jo Brand is fat.*

And that was it.

Probably
off my face
on something

*Above:* Trying to get off with a statue of James Joyce

*Right:* Doing a very good impression of a tower in Ireland

*Below:* In Tasmania with friend Gabe (right) and Tour Manager John (left). Guess who's worked in security?

*Above:* Emergency Clinic Christmas reunion. Yes, some of us are catatonically pissed

*Below:* Thinking about my next lie down

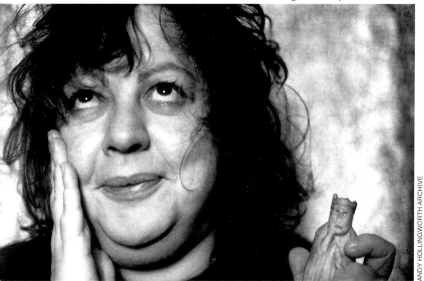

ANDY HOLLINGWORTH ARCHIVE

*Above:* In bed with Jarvis Cocker having a fag after… having another fag

*Below:* Publicity shot for *Mental* with mate Griffo. We're laughing because we're mad and menopausal

*Inset:* Just before I sobered up. Montreal Rapids

*Main photo:* In Montreal about to drown. Some arse has made me sit at the front

OFF THE KERB PRODUCTIONS PRESENTS

# JO BRAND

## 'A carbuncle on the hard-earned face of feminism'
Mail On Sunday

WITH SPECIAL GUEST **ANDY ROBINSON**

**'The comedy equivalent of gold dust'**
The Guardian

**MAY**

| | | |
|---|---|---|
| 6th | **PORTSMOUTH** Guildhall | 01705 824355 |
| 7th | **GUILDFORD** Civic Hall | 01483 444555 |
| 9th | **COVENTRY** Warwick Arts Centre | 01203 524524 |
| 11th | **OXFORD** Apollo | 01865 244544 |
| 14th | **WATFORD** Colosseum | 01923 445000 |
| 15th | **MANCHESTER** Bridgewater Hall | 0161 907 9000 |
| 16th | **LIVERPOOL** Philharmonic | 0151 709 3789 |
| 17th | **HULL** City Hall | 01482 226655 |
| 18th | **PRESTON** Guildhall | 01772 258858 |
| 20th | **CAMBRIDGE** Corn Exchange | 01223 357851 |
| 21st | **WOLVERHAMPTON** Civic Hall | 01902 312030 |
| 22nd | **BRADFORD** St George's Hall | 01274 752000 |
| 23rd | **YORK** Barbican Centre | 01904 656688 |
| 24th | **MIDDLESBOROUGH** Town Hall | 01642 242561 |
| 25th | **NOTTINGHAM** Royal Centre | 0115 9482626 |
| 28th | **BOURNEMOUTH** Pavilion | 01202 456456 |
| 29th | **BIRMINGHAM** Symphony Hall | 0121 2123333 |
| 30th | **SHEFFIELD** City Hall | 0114 2789789 |
| 31st | **NEWCASTLE** Tyne Theatre | 0191 232 0899 |

**JUNE**

| | | |
|---|---|---|
| 1st | **LEICESTER** De Montfort Hall | 0116 2333111 |
| 2nd | **HIGH WYCOMBE** Swan | 512000 |
| 4th | **IPSWICH** Regent | 01473 1480 |
| 5th | **NORWICH** Theatre Royal | 01603 6 00 |
| 7th | **SWANSEA** Grand Theatre | 01 |
| 8th | **CARDIFF** St David's Hall | 22 878 1 |
| 9th | **BRISTOL** Colston Hall  01 | 922 6/cc922236 |
| 10th | **CHELTENHAM** Town Hall | 01242 22797 |
| 11th | **SALISBURY** City Hall | 01722 327676 |
| 12th | **BASINGSTOKE** Anvil | 01256 844244 |
| 13th | **BEDFORD** Corn Exchange | 01234 269519 |

DESIGN **tangerine** PHOTO TIM O'SULLIVAN

Mmm – really comfy!

*Above:* Normally I block out the entire slogan

*Below:* And The Comedy Store did eat me up…many times

ANDY HOLLINGWORTH ARCHIVE

ANDY HOLLINGWORTH ARCHIVE

Threatening to fall on
the front ten rows

**Third Edinburgh, 1990**

My third Edinburgh was also as part of a trio. Patrick Marber, James Macabre and I styled ourselves as a band, The Holy Cardigans. Each of us did a stand-up bit and came together at the end as a musical combo. In terms of who did what, the only true musician amongst us was Jim (James Macabre), who played guitar. Patrick couldn't play anything so he had to be the lead singer, and I played keyboards very badly, since having given up the piano when I was twelve, I was pretty crap.

We were at the Gilded Balloon, in a small sweaty room with a low ceiling. By this point I was having an on-off relationship with Jim, which didn't make things particularly easy. He was more serious about the music than me and Patrick, who were just mucking about. There were many dirty looks slung across the stage as I plodded very badly through my keyboard part like a depressed Liberace. (Hey! Google him, kids!)

I shared a rented flat with Jim and a couple of other comics. There was endless partying and a constant stream of comics in and out, day and night. Our downstairs neighbour, a man who I think worked on a building site, must have been driven mad by it. He used to leave his heavy work boots outside his front door, and one day someone, on their way down from our flat after a marathon partying session, strolled past his flat and nicked them.

I assume this was just some sort of silly prank and not meant maliciously, but the owner of the boots went absolutely mental. We were woken by the most terrifying banging on the door at about seven in the morning, to be confronted by one of the angriest people I have ever seen – and having worked in a Psychiatric Emergency Clinic, that's saying some-thing. He was incandescent with rage and I honestly thought he was going to beat the shit out of us, if not kill us. Of course, the boys' attempts to reason with him just added fuel to the fire, and he left saying that if his boots weren't back there by the evening or some money to replace them, he would 'fucking kill' us.

I sheepishly poked some money through his door, praying he was not in and would not come to the door to 'thank' me.

## Fourth Edinburgh, 1992
Against my natural instinct, I was persuaded for my next Edinburgh to strike out on my own, and was offered an hour in the aforementioned posh-sounding Supper Room at the Assembly Rooms. I say 'against my natural

instinct' because I have always preferred to be on a bill with other comics.

This is for two reasons.

Firstly, I am a gregarious person and I like being with other people. This means you can chat in the dressing room, discuss the audience and all go home together and get pissed afterwards, whereas the solo gigs I have done tend to have been rather lonely affairs . . . especially if I'd had a bad one.

Secondly, doing a show on your own demands so much material – a whole hour or more. Now I know some stand-ups manage to blah on for ever, but I am not one of them. My material tends to be fairly spare and one-liner-ish. I envy those comics who can ramble at will in a conversational style as it seems to fill up much more time. I was approaching this Edinburgh with, if I'm honest, only forty minutes of material, and I needed an hour.

So I decided to pad it out with songs. This wasn't a great idea for someone who can't sing very well. Comedy songs are always a bit risky anyway, although if you incorporate up-to-the-minute topical material, that seems to give them a bit of a boost.

Subtlety was never my strong point and the songs used to get big laughs or gasps, either of which was acceptable to me so that was how it had to be. Weirdly, as I wasn't particularly pleased with the show I was doing, I got nominated for the Perrier Award, a comedy gong for what a panel of judges considered to be the best stand-up/comedy show.

The nominees for the award my year were:

Me
Steve Coogan and John Thomson
Mark Thomas
Bruce Morton
John Shuttleworth (real name Graham Fellows)

I didn't think I had the slightest chance of winning but nursed the dream that I would, by some quirk of fate, receive the ultimate accolade. On the actual night I was unable to attend the party, which I was secretly relieved about, because I'm not a big fan of awards ceremonies. It's not that I can't make a nice face and be genuinely pleased for the person who has won, I'm happy to do that. There is just something I don't like about the atmosphere of them. Normally they are a bit boring, people are pissed and annoying, and I'd rather be at home watching telly.

So I deliberately agreed to a live radio interview on

Radio Forth and asked one of the organisers to give me a ring when the prize was announced at about 11 p.m. so I knew one way or the other.

Well, I'm sitting there talking bollocks like one does on those sorts of radio shows and the clock ticked tortuously past the time of the announcement. I received no message and then the news came on – at which point they announced that the winners were Steve Coogan and John Thomson.

I had known Steve and John for a while by then. I met John Thomson with Mark Lamarr when we did a gig up in Manchester and he was on the bill. We all did OK. John was an impressionist at the time but had tried very hard to turn people's expectations on their head. For example, he did a very good impression of Bernard Manning, which started as if he was going to do the usual Manning type of racist material and have a go at one ethnic group or another, but at the last minute he would flip it upside down and say he had used the ethnic groups to illustrate cultural harmony. The character's name was 'Bernard Right On'.

When I first met John I found him a bit cocky and irritating. He was really young at the time, barely twenty and too in-yer-face. However, over the years he's turned into a really good laugh, a nice bloke and fun to be with. I don't see him that often, but when I do it's always really great to catch up. I had a huge laugh with him on *Fame Academy* and I found the tabloid hounding of him some years ago really distasteful and undeserved. (It's not like journalists don't fill themselves full of booze and drugs, bloody hypocrites.)

I always thought Steve Coogan was a huge talent right from the kick-off. He was a brilliant mimic and his characters were marvellous. My favourite was the student-hating Paul Calf who would slag off anyone and anything in his orbit.

So I found out I hadn't won the Perrier Award live on the radio . . . slightly disconcerting, but still infinitely preferable to being there. The interviewer probed for signs of disappointment, envy and homicidal feelings, but to be honest, there weren't any. I was genuinely pleased for John and Steve whose show was brilliant – so that was the end of that.

However, my show sold out every night, and to me that is a better indicator of success than getting some daft award. Also, at this point, I was beginning to be recognised on the street by people, and as most people in Edinburgh are pissed for the whole three weeks of the Festival, they let me know in no uncertain terms by shouting, trying to kiss me or just aiming some abuse in my direction. I suppose it was at this point I began to curtail my social life. Whereas before I had been pretty relaxed about going into any old pub, I now tended to hang around places that were slightly exclusive like the Assembly Rooms bar, because you needed some sort of pass to get in. It sounds wanky, I know, but in all honesty it did make life easier because I knew I would bump into someone there that I knew and could talk to, and hopefully the sort of people who would try to ruin my life would not be allowed in.

I chose to lay off Edinburgh for a bit after that. The pressure of writing enough fresh material to persuade the critics that I had an entirely new show was too strong and I decided it was better not to bother.

I did, however, go up to Edinburgh for a one-off show at the Playhouse a couple of years later. The Playhouse is massive, seating about 3,000. Mark Lamarr was compering and there was a line-up of the most fashionable comedians around at the time. Memories of this show include Mark Lamarr coming on stage with absolutely no clothes on whatsoever – much to the delight of the audience.

But sometimes you can die on stage. This might happen to a comic at any time, even when they are storming the gig and surfing on a wave of undying love.

It's such a fine line in comedy between laughs and boos sometimes, and it all hinges on such trivial things.

I made a big mistake in Scotland one night. A two-part gig to raise money for charity had been arranged so that a set of comics did two gigs, one in Edinburgh and one in Glasgow on the same night. It's about a forty-five minute trip between the two. I did Edinburgh first and then hopped in a car and set off for Glasgow. Glasgow audiences are mythically difficult and there have been many legends about comics dying horrible deaths at the Glasgow Empire. It did not exist by the time my generation got round to working in Glasgow, but the residual fear still remained.

The night's auspices weren't good, due to my suffering from what many people think is the mythical PMT but is very real in many women's cases. I was bad-tempered, slightly paranoid and one of my favourite words, 'labile' – a term used often in psychiatry to denote someone who is emotionally on the edge and could lose it at any time. Not a good state to be in when facing a pissed Glasgow audience, at any rate.

When I stepped on stage, someone shouted something along the lines of, 'Fuck off, you fat English cow!' and it pretty soon slipped into warfare. Normally I would have used my ascending collection of pre-prepared put-downs, but I was in no mood and launched straight in with a couple of my mega-put-downs which were very coarse and aggressive. This unfortunately did not do the trick, and to my incredulity, after some very bad-tempered banter between us about the Scots and the English, I found myself saying, 'Well, who the fuck won at Culloden?'

As soon as the words had come out of my mouth I knew this was A VERY BIG MISTAKE.

As if the atmosphere wasn't bad enough already, it then descended further down the scale of civilisation and became really dark. However, as PMT sufferers might tell you, in a weird way this was somewhat enjoyable in a masochistic sense, and I stayed on longer, taking a right verbal kicking and only leaving the stage when I thought it looked likely that someone might jump up there and take a swing at me.

I take full responsibility for this furore. It was totally my fault and I deserved what I got. It is just slightly scary that when faced with a semi-baying mob I decided not to go down the Mrs Sensible route but crank things up even more. Glasgow, I apologise. I have always loved Scotland and regret turning into a British bulldog for five seconds.

## Another Edinburgh, 2003

After a substantial break of a few years in which I got married and had two children (more of this elsewhere), I had another crack at Edinburgh. We decided to go up as a family and rented a house there. Eliza was six months old and Maisie one and a half.

I took on a bit too much as I was doing my own hour-long stand-up show at 10.45 in the big venue at the Assembly Rooms, after performing a two-hander play with my friend Helen Griffin, or 'Griffo', in a smaller venue there. The play was called *Mental*, and Griffo and I had written it together. It was about a psychiatric nurse and a patient and was set at night. The trick at the beginning was that we didn't make it clear who was the patient and who was the nurse, and tried to make some points about mental health in a funny and not too worthy way.

I had known Griffo since university and we'd both trained as psychiatric nurses, whilst also nursing ambitions – hers to become an actor and mine to go into comedy.

Griffo has had a tougher time than me in the world of acting. Firstly, it is much more competitive and there are many actors competing for any one job. Griffo moved back to Wales reasonably early on in her career and I think this has enabled her to be a big fish in a small pond. *Doctor Who* buffs may know her from the Tennant/Cybermen battle episodes in which she played a revolutionary van-driving underground type called Mrs Moore.

Doing the Edinburgh Festival with the family in tow was a very different prospect from doing Edinburgh as a single woman. Most of the differences can be summed up under the heading 'responsibility'. Whereas during previous Edinburghs I could party till dawn and get off my face, I was now pretty much waking up at dawn and therefore wanting to go to bed about ten, which was forty-five minutes before my stand-up show even started. I found it bloody difficult and stressful, especially given that Griffo and I had to perform our play first. Days were spent out with the kids, maybe at the beach – but although it's beautiful, the nearest beach at North Berwick tends to have a gale-force wind blowing across it, making a mouthful of sand a certainty and frostbite a distinct possibility.

My social life dwindled to nothing, as by the time I finished my stand-up show at 11.45 I would have been quite happy to fall over backwards onto the stage and start snoring there and then. Still, I got through it without having some sort of showbiz 'breakdown' and vowed never to do two shows back to back ever again.

Griffo and I got pretty good reviews for the play and as we neared the end of the three-week run I got slightly stir crazy and planned a joke for the last night.

In the play there was a line which Griffo had to say: 'You wouldn't expect a man in a fucking bear costume to walk in, would you?'

I managed to persuade one of the guys who was doing a show before us to dress up in a bear costume and enter stage right when Griffo said that line. Unfortunately, the audience was completely confused as to why someone had actually appeared dressed as a bear, and Griffo was – to put it mildly – *not amused*. I suppose this underlines the differences between stand-ups and actresses. I just wanted to make her laugh. She, on the other hand, just wanted to do her job. Another of my practical jokes gone wrong.

Still, we got over it. I apologised profusely and things got back to normal. I crawled back to London, exhausted and jaded, and hoped I would never do Edinburgh again.

I *have* done Edinburgh since, but pretty much as a one-off or doing a benefit. I suppose it might be a possibility when the kids are older, but by that time I plan to be in a bath-chair on Hastings seafront.

## Brief Diary Entries During Edinburgh, 2003

Hunting back through my old diaries, I discovered that I had somehow managed to scrawl some thoughts about how it was all going, when I did the *Mental* play and my own stand-up, and the kids were babies.

*Friday 1 August*
Press launch . . . hideous. *Mental*: sold out.
Restrained but good laughs. Shaky on some
lines. Stand-up show: hard but fair and a laugh.

*Saturday 2 August*
*Mental*: sold out. Really good crowd. Laughed
uproariously in places. Our prop walkie-talkies
picking up security. Stand-up: the bastards criti-
cised my clothes!

*Sunday 3 August*
*Mental*: sold out. Big tech hitches and Griffo
early wobbler. Nice audience. Stand-Up: bunch
of 300 twats.

*Monday 4 August*
Day off. Hoofuckingray.

*Tuesday 5 August*
*Mental*: sold out. Terrible arseholes in front row.
Stand-up: heckle agogo.

*Wednesday 6 August*
*Mental*: good. Stand-up: stilted, unpleasant.

*Thursday 7 August*
*Mental*: Couldn't find our way out. [No idea
what this means.] No laughs. Stand-Up: very
good crowd, no weirdies. 2 people left near the
end. [Oh madam, the insecurity.]

*Friday 8 August*
*Mental*: sold out. Good, v good. Stand-up: sold
out. Oh shit, Friday night, full of pissed bonkers
barmies.

*Saturday 9 August*
*Mental*: sold out. Stand-up: sold out.

*[Didn't write anything at all for Sunday 10 August.]*

*Monday 11 August*
Day off. Jesus, am bloody knackered.

*Tuesday 12 August*
*Mental*: bloody hard graft till halfway point then
the buggers lightened up a bit. Stand-up: sold out.

*Wednesday 13 August*
*Mental*: bit of a struggle. Stand-up: dull – me,
not them.

*Thursday 14 August*
*Mental*: a hard, grinding pisser of a show.
Stand-up: best so far.

*Friday 15 August*
*Mental*: sold out, really good fun. Standup: good
fun. The bastards made me sing.

*Saturday 16 August*
*Mental*: good. Stand-up: fucking hard work.

*Sunday 17 August*
*Mental*: sour audience, Griffo fell on me. Stand-up:
wading through bloody concrete.

*Monday 18 August*
Barely alive. Day off.

*Tuesday 19 August*
*Mental*: Griffo had TB type coughing fit.
Stand-up: fucking hard work.

*Wednesday 20 August*
*Mental*: dull, dull, dull, dull. Stand-up: audience
full of personality disorders.

*Thursday 21 August*
*Mental*: no breaking-glass sound effect, just
weird click. Stand-up: did as benefit, very
nice.

*Friday 22 August*
*Mental*: nice crowd, but we were bloody
shambolic. I forgot lines, Griffo got her knitting
caught. Stand-up: they were evil and should be
killed.

*Saturday 23 August*
*Mental*: so knackered, felt I was on auto. Played

bear trick on Griffo – not impressed, oh no.
Stand-up: they were pissed, me too.

*Sunday 24 August*
Hooray . . . it's over.

# BEING JO BRAND

# Being Clocked

Being recognised is a progressive phenomenon which doesn't really dawn on you until it's pretty much under way. I suppose the first time should have been a big event in my life, but I can't even remember when it was. And it was very gradual too, with maybe two or three months between the first and second time.

It also catches you unawares. In the chemist, in the street, and when you least want it.

At first, people's recognition is hazy; they are not absolutely sure who you are, so they take a stab in the dark. This is when you tend to get an array of mistaken identities and double-takes as you walk down the street. Some people come back and check. Then there are the surreptitious ones who walk past you and do a double-take, and then do an about-turn and try to wander back past you as naturally as possible, while staring at you – and you can almost see the neurones firing in their brains. Other, bolder ones will march right back up to you like the police, stick their face in yours and demand, 'Who are you?' Some people just think they know you and say hello as they pass; I always give a cheery hello back.

Others turn it into a quiz. 'No, don't tell me, hang on . . . I do know you, don't I? It's Jo Something, isn't it. No, *don't* tell me' – sometimes they get quite cross – and you have to stand there like a nana while they desperately try and identify you. Others will take a stab at a name that fits roughly into one's area of entertainment.

My top five wrong identities are:

1. A bloke behind the counter in a record shop in Devon, who said, 'You're a famous dancer, aren't you?' Bloody hell, when have you ever seen a dancer who was several stone overweight? Maybe he thought I was one of Les Dawson's famed troupe of dancers, the Roly Polys.

2. Someone said to me once: 'Ruby Wax, hi! Can I have your autograph?' I did a complete scribble that was unrecognisable as a name to save their embarrassment. I also texted Ruby, who I'm sure wasn't very flattered as she is half my size.

3. Also on several occasions I have been identified as Dawn French. Very flattered, frankly.

4. Once identified as 'a newsreader'. Mmm yes – Huw Edwards, that's me.

5. I once went into a shop in a small town in Wales and the elderly guy behind the counter said, 'I've no idea who you are, but I heard you were in town.'

The upside of being recognised for me is that people are usually really nice and friendly. It may be the case that if people can't stand you, then they don't bother to come up and say hello, which is fine by me. I'd rather have that than a mouthful of abuse.

Once people do know who you are, if you don't like to be constantly approached, there are several options:

- Never go out. This is an option for some, but not for me. I think that once you have children, you owe it to them to try and give them as normal a life as possible, and this involves getting stuck into ordinary life. It can be difficult at times as it's hard for me when I'm with the children and people come up for autographs etc. But it's preferable to not taking on those day-to-day tasks which are all part of normal life.

- Go out in disguise. I have experimented with a selection of disguises, but it seems that donning a big hat or silly coat doesn't fool anyone. (I have tried both these.) A bloke in a shop in Tottenham Court Road in London once said to me, 'You can take that stupid hat off; we all know who you are.' He went on to tell me that Chris Evans goes unnoticed whenever he comes into the shop. Apart from by you, mate, obviously.

- Make a plan which avoids major areas of potential hassle.

For me, places where schoolchildren congregate are always a threat as the peer-group phenomenon gives them false courage. So I don't tend to hang round secondary schools. And as I don't need to, that's fairly easy.

When we had snow one winter, I was walking down the road when I came upon a group of teenage boys chucking snowballs at cars. Oh, here we go, I thought, there's one with my name on it. I decided to wrong-foot them as I saw one of the boys raise a snowball-filled hand and started to run towards them, shouting, 'What are you going to do with *that*?' (Plus some swearing.)

Thankfully, it worked and the snowball was dropped on the road. I then attempted a completely ridiculous plea for them to stop throwing snowballs at cars, especially cars with old ladies in them, pointing out that they could be responsible for killing someone and go to prison, which of course was 99 per cent bullshit. They looked at me with the teenage boy stare, half defiant, half empty brain-ish. And then I marched off with as much dignity as I could muster, which to be honest with you is not much at all. As I walked on down the road I was aware of a quiet crunching behind me and thought, Oh, here we go again. Now I'm going to get a snowball in the back of the head. I turned to see two of the boys looking rather sheepish. 'Sorry,' they mumbled. Bloody hell, result.

The worst places for me are pubs, clubs or crowded areas on a Friday night when everyone is pissed in a tired, irritable and lary way. I do much crossing of streets with my head down, I dive into shop doorways or go into shops, I squat on the pavement to do up an imaginary shoelace or I face a wall for no reason, which in itself must look pretty stupid. But these minor tactics have served me well and I have had relatively little hassle over the years.

My biggest mistakes have been:

- Drinking in a huge hotel bar in Belfast on a Friday night. First of all I met a singer who was very big in the eighties, completely off his face, who made a beeline for me, arms out and breathing red-wine fumes right at me, while he announced with pride, 'I've just come out of rehab today!' He was followed by an even drunker bloke who forced his way onto our table, sat on my lap, drank my drink, snatched my fag out of my mouth and then tried to stick his tongue in there instead. At this point John, my tour manager, manhandled him off me and escorted him a few feet away while I regretted the hideous drunken kiss and felt sick.

- I once agreed to meet someone in a pub and they were late. As I tried to sit quietly in a corner looking at my watch and pretending to read a piece of paper I had in my bag, which was a shopping list, I became a pisshead magnet and every single inebriated individual in the pub gradually came and sat down at the table, saying as they always do, 'You're fucking loaded, buy us a drink.' Eventually, I could stand it no longer, made my excuses about going to the lav and legged it from the pub, never to return. I have no objection, by the way, to buying anyone a drink. However, I do have an objection to sitting there and drinking it with them if they are pissed out of their heads and talking utter bollocks at me.

- This was something that I couldn't have avoided, but I found myself on a plane from Dublin to London sitting right behind a very pissed rugby team. I didn't want them to recognise me as I knew I would get it big time, so I spent the entire flight with my hands over my face, staring down towards the floor and looking like I was seriously depressed. I was desperate for a piss as well, but the agony of getting up and being clocked was a far worse prospect than being incontinent.

There are also places in Central London where it is advisable not to go unless you like having your picture taken by the paps. These are top fashionable restaurants or showbiz haunts like The Ivy, where several paps hang about outside 24/7 in the vain hope they will catch Cilla Black with a big bogey hanging out of her nose or one of Girls Aloud with her pants showing. Also, film premières are not a great idea – unless you want to run the gauntlet of rows of paps shouting, 'Over 'ere, Jo!' 'To me! To me!' 'Over 'ere, you silly cow!' and other delightful stuff like that.

I was once at a party with my best friend's husband Roland (yes, she did know) and I was approached by a slightly histrionic PR woman who said her client's car had not turned up and would I give this celeb a lift in my car. She meant my chauffeur-driven car, but I always drive myself. I agreed to do it, picked up my car from round the corner and then discovered my cab fare was Jermaine Jackson. What a hoot.

We were ushered outside the stage door and as we appeared, it all went mental. Jermaine Jackson and his wife were pushed into the back of the car and Roland

and I got in the front. At this point we were surrounded by about thirty paps and a few had actually got on the bonnet of the car. I have to say it gave me great pleasure to turn on the ignition and pull away, sloughing off a couple of them onto the pavement as I went. Jermaine Jackson was a sweet, almost childlike person, very softly spoken and unerringly polite. We dropped him at a posh hotel and he kindly allowed me to take a picture of him and Roland on my mobile phone. It gave me a very interesting insight into the life of mega-stars like him. Poor sod, I really would never go out if I got that level of attention.

Most people say that if you are famous you have to put up with the side-effects because that's what you wanted. Fair enough, but I do feel one should be accorded some privacy at those times of one's life when we all expect it.

Having a baby is one of those times and I found it difficult that I got weird attention during that period. It is true (as I mention on stage) that someone did actually come into the labour suite while I was in the middle of things, as it were, and ask for my autograph. This is bad enough, but the fact that it was a doctor, to me made it even worse.

I was once at our local hospital in the Outpatients

Department waiting for an appointment. As usual I was in a corner, face in a magazine trying to be unobtrusive when a nurse – in her fifties, I would estimate – came and stood next to me, pointed down at my head and shouted, 'Look everyone, it's that comedian off the telly!' God, I was so embarrassed I didn't know what to do for the best. I smiled weakly and just hoped she'd piss off. However, she went and got a piece of paper and made a big show of getting my autograph. So much for patient confidentiality.

I suppose when I'm out and about it is sensible to expect one or two people to recognise me and to be prepared and have my nice face on. Although we're all the same and some days we don't feel like putting a nice face on, I just have to work a bit harder.

I do draw the line at some things and I was a bit pissed off when I had been at the local dry cleaner's to discover that some silly cow of a journalist had been standing behind me and noted down all the items I'd handed in for cleaning. Her article appeared in the paper the next day. Not only that, she'd taken the piss out of my clothes and remarked on how inappropriate they were for a woman of my age. I didn't exactly hand in a gimp mask and a fur bikini so I don't know what she was on about. Revenge is a dish best eaten cold they say and I'm sure our paths will cross at some point in the future and enable me to remonstrate in my own, very special way.

# 'Ladies' and 'Gentlemen' of the Press (Including Yours Truly)

The fundamental problem I think we have with the press is one of competing perspectives. Many people assume that the newspapers are there to report the actual news. In fact, this doesn't seem to be true, because lots of newspapers are just comics for grown-ups and are there to entertain rather than inform. Also, each newspaper's output is dictated, firstly, by whoever the owner is, and secondly, whoever the Editor is.

I don't think it even occurs to a lot of people how

obsessionally selective different papers are about what is 'the news' and how they present it. So, one also finds a strong political perspective in papers, which is kind of hidden beneath the surface under the guise of faithful news reporting. And as most people tend to buy a paper which buoys up and expresses their views, they just end up reading what they want to hear.

My interactions with the press can be categorised as:

1. *Unsolicited articles or papped photos.*
2. *Prearranged interviews to promote particular projects.*
3. *The vile, vomitous outpourings of self-regulated monsters. Oh, I beg your pardon, that's not very objective of me. I mean, of course, TV critics.*

Let's start with unsolicited articles that are beyond one's control. This can be pretty frustrating and my approach is to ignore them. There's nothing you can do about it, so why worry? On occasion, people I know will mention they have seen an article and then I am compelled to read it, because I have to know what's in it. These tend only to be bad. Is there an element of schadenfreude in their action of informing me about a nasty article? Who knows? Freud would have us believe that much of what we do and our motives are fuelled by our unconscious, so I like to think that so-called friends don't consciously relish my distress at great big slag-offs of my work and me.

The slag-offs, it has to be said, were and are in the *Daily Mail* mostly, apart from tabloid glee at occasional faux pas or me looking particularly bad. That is because I became, owing to the material I did and the way I dressed, a byword for unfeminine, bolshie, unwashed, man-hating, aggressive womanhood. Therefore, fairly frequently I would be held up as an example of what I shall call 'What Not to Be' – against the perfect *Mail* woman who was well-dressed, submissive, right-wing and domesticated.

I once saw an article (yes, one that 'a friend' had told me about) in which someone – can't remember who – was held up as a paragon of virtue for *Mail* readers in terms of her appearance, whereas they had found a picture of me looking like a right old scruffbag with the delightful accompanying caption: *Jo Brand: Doesn't care.*

On the whole I have managed to steer clear of 'the paps' who only appear on the great occasions in one's life like marriages and births. I was followed around once when I was making *Through the Cakehole*. I'd been driving through South London on my way to a meeting in the centre of London when I became aware of a car behind me. I think for women drivers this can be a relatively frequent occurrence: you have to establish whether you are being followed and if so, take evasive action. In these cases I tend to turn off down side-streets and wiggle about a bit to see if the car behind stays with me.

On that day when I thought I was being followed I did exactly that. I drove a rather circuitous route to my meeting and realised after ten minutes that matey was still with me. My competitive nature dictates I find it hard to let these people get the better of me, so as I pulled up outside the meeting-place I was ready to jump out of the car and leg it immediately and got in through the door of Channel X before he'd even got out of the car.

When I came out with a couple of other people, matey was still there. He obviously had no idea I'd clocked him. We went into the pub opposite and sat by the window so I could see what he was doing. Sure enough, he got out of the car and started to head towards the pub. As he came in through the door, I exited through another, jumped in the car and drove off, giving him a wave as he ran out of the pub. I know this is a tiny incident and it means very little, but it used to give me a huge sense of achievement to escape. Pathetic really on my part.

When I got engaged I was followed a bit and when I got married I kept it quiet so was not followed at all.

However, when the *Sun* did find out I'd got married they allotted me a very charming headline on the front of the paper which read, *Here Comes the Bride, All Fat and Wide!* I can't tell you how touched I was by that.

I also had a couple of paps outside the house after I came home from the hospital with my first baby. Apart from that, it seems paps are lazy. Unless you are on the Madonna/Cheryl Cole/Wayne Rooney level of fame they don't put themselves out, which is good. The only other time one tends to get papped is at restaurants where celebs go, or at awards ceremonies.

I suppose my only pappation that I noticed was many years ago when I came out of The Ivy, a showbiz restaurant I try to avoid, and the photographer asked me to put my bag in front of my face. Charming! I sneered in his general direction and he begged, saying he hadn't sold a picture for ages. Gullible twat that I am, I acquiesced and sure enough, in the *News of the World* the following Sunday, there appeared a picture of me with my bag over my face and next to it a picture of Princess Diana with her bag over her face and the headline *Which One of These is a Princess?* Well, me, obviously.

I've never moved in the showbiz/royalty social circle, maybe because I'm a republican. I've turned down the Royal Variety Performance on a number of occasions because I feel it's hypocritical to call for the abolition of the monarchy and then go to a show and curtsey to Her Maj.

I did, however, meet Diana once on *The Clive James Show* (I believe that she and Clive James were friends). When I got to the show there was a lot of whispering and barely controlled hysteria going on. One of the runners informed me, 'We've got a very important guest coming down to watch the show.'

'Who is it?' I asked.

'I can't tell you,' he replied.

'Oh, go on,' I said.

'Oh, all right,' he replied. 'It's Princess Diana.'

Blimey, he would have made a really crap spy.

On the show we were doing an item about food

with rude names in other languages. For example, I had some chewing gum called *Spunk* which a friend had sent me from Germany. I brought it along with me to the show and did a joke about spitting it out. (Yes, sorry, I know.)

After the show had finished, we all ended up in the green room and were told we would be introduced to the Princess. Stephen Fry was there and began to instruct me in royal etiquette, showing me how to curtsey. I maintained that I would not curtsey for a royal. He also remarked as she moved along the queue that he was dying for a wee. I wondered aloud why he didn't just go. Apparently it's not considered good manners to leave the room when royalty's in. Better to wet yourself then.

Diana reached me in the queue and I resisted a curtsey and just shook hands. She bent over towards me conspiratorially and said, 'Loved your chewing-gum joke.' We had a laugh about some of the names and she moved on. Her interest did seem genuinely natural and unforced. Poor cow, I felt sorry for her. I think it's really hard to keep that smile on your face as endless individuals pass excitedly past you, come rain or shine. It requires a certain sort of personality and charm, and Diana certainly seemed to have it. And how ironic in a culture that worships beautiful women that old jug ears was secretly in love with someone not considered traditionally attractive. Good on her – us non-beauties are heartily sick of the endless droning on about women's looks.

Prearranged interviews with newspapers, or interviews on telly, or radio interviews are a necessary evil to promote whatever one's current project is. There are obviously a handful of iconic cult figures who never grant interviews and who don't seem to give a shit whether the public buy what they have to offer or not. I very much admire these people, but I do not emulate them because we have a family to support and a mortgage to pay.

Over the years I have tried to steer clear of the papers I don't like very much, but in the good old, bad old days it wasn't like that. I thought I had to do everything. I once did a photo-shoot for *Cosmopolitan* which went with an accompanying little piece about 'up-and-coming comic', etc etc. The article itself was pretty harmless, but the photo session was excruciating and involved me having to squat on a high stool for about forty minutes looking like I was enjoying it. After about five minutes I couldn't feel my feet and was desperate to say 'Fuck this, I'm off.' However, at that point, I didn't realise I could actually say no to things, and the residual well of politeness, which I had had poured onto my grey-matter as a child, prevented me.

An interview with the *Daily Mail* was similarly painful. It was quite early on, when I didn't understand that their editorial line on me was as an unacceptable, probably lesbian nightmare. Following a pretty friendly interview, the ensuing article ripped me apart. It taught me a valuable lesson though, and at that point I became much more wary of the way various journalists would portray me.

In reality, what it comes down to in interviews is what the journalist thinks of you as a person and the line they have been instructed to take editorially. So, it doesn't matter how polite, how entertaining, how solicitous you are, if they have decided to be horrible to you, horrible they will be.

Added to this, over the years I have read so much sneering journalism about celebrities' houses that I will never let a journalist set foot in my house unless I have a contract killer waiting in the cupboard to finish them off. And believe you me, that thought has crossed my mind more than once.

\*     \*     \*

The critic is a strange animal. To assume that your opinion is more valuable than anyone else's surely makes you a bit of a big-headed twat. And this opinion has been borne out on more occasions than I care to remember. Again, it comes down to the paper's editorial line, coupled with the critic's personal opinion of you. I know for a fact that I have done gigs which I absolutely stormed and the audience loved, and have consequently been completely rubbished by a critic as if I died on my arse. And the more vile and personal a critic is about you, the more the readers of those august organs like the *Sun* and the *Mail* enjoy it.

There is no such thing as an objective critic. They unavoidably bring their personality, prejudices and taste to their pieces of work, regardless of what an audience thinks or what the ratings say. This can work positively in some cases, such as if a comedian is doing horrible racist or misogynist material and the critic is offended, but on the whole, randomness seems a big weapon in their arsenal. You don't know if they were in a bad mood when they watched you, had just had a row with their partner, don't like fat women, don't like left-wingers. It's impossible to fathom.

And there's no defence. Letters to papers berating critics or journalists inevitably look whining and pathetic.

I'm not saying all negative criticism is bad, it can be constructive and help you change direction, but when it's a tirade of personal abuse, that's different.

I got it with both barrels from the critics very early on and became slightly obsessed with it. Of course I don't want to give him any more publicity than he deserves, which is none, but a certain critic in the *Sun* took against me quite early on and directed a stream of abuse about my appearance at *Sun* readers. The only way I could counter this was in my act, by saying that he wasn't exactly an oil painting himself – unless there was an oil painting called *Constipated Warthog Licking Piss Off a Toilet Seat*. Well, it made me feel better.

Another critic, who works for the *Evening Standard* and who is considered a bit of a wit, although much of his copy is crap, once remarked that I should be sent to Saudi Arabia where they know how to deal with extra pounds of ugly flesh. However, I do derive a great deal of satisfaction from the fact that his comedy career amounted to nothing after a couple of crappy series on telly.

I know I'm making it sound as if all journalists are psychopaths, and that's not true. There are some good 'uns – it's just I've never met any.

Thanks, dear reader for allowing me to cathart.

## Newspaper Columns: The Endless Search for an Original Thought

When your profile enters the public domain, people start to want to know your opinion on things, and opinion is a huge part of what newspapers and newspaper columnists do.

In the nineties, when I was asked whether I wanted to write a column for the *Independent*, I was somewhat wary since, because of their very nature, newspaper columns just seem to be a long list of celebrity character assassinations.

There was, of course, the late Lynda Lee-Potter in the *Mail* who made it her stock in trade to be absolutely vile, mainly about other women's looks, and I didn't want to end up doing that as I think the majority of women get enough disdain in the pages of the tabloids without me joining in. Lynda, who died in 2004, was forever immortalised in *Private Eye* as Glenda Slagg, and I always used to think the spoof column in that brilliant satirical magazine was so well-observed. Perhaps her most shameful hour was when she set to work on the glorious Mo Mowlam, the late Labour politician, describing her as looking like a Geordie trucker. This is the kind of abuse I'd expect from a yob on the street who is ill-educated and misogynistic, but to see it in print written by another woman made my blood boil. So I made a supreme effort not to have a go at the appearance of women and concentrate, for example, on their political views rather than how they looked, while generally promoting commonsense all round.

It's easier said than done, having to drag up opinions on a regular basis. Some weeks I would sit and look at my computer screen, empty and sad, and think to myself, What the feck do I think about anything this week? I would pray for interesting things to happen to me so I could talk about them.

For a period of time, Janet Street Porter was Editor of the *Independent* and I found her fierceness very entertaining because underneath I think she's a decent person. But one week, after a call from Janet, I foolishly agreed to give a plug to some charity thing Elton John was doing (they are good friends) even though I felt uncomfortable about it.

Rightly so, a little piece about it appeared in *Private Eye* under the heading of *Brown-nosing*. I felt suitably admonished. Eventually, my column was syndicated to the *Daily Mirror* and suitably tabloided up for *Mirror* readers. I found that quite difficult to look at. I eventually resigned from the *Mirror* after what I considered to be a racist front page, and hoped Piers Morgan's career would head downhill. Well, that hasn't happened, has it?

# Corporate Gigs and Getting Gongs

As one's star rises so, it seems, does one's currency in the world of 'corporate entertainment'. This covers anything that pertains to professions and businesses providing entertainment or awards for their employees. Traditionally, these companies have a fair bit of money to throw about, so they pay extremely well on a sliding scale depending on how popular/famous you are.

I quite like doing corporates, not necessarily for the obvious pecuniary reasons, but because they tend to be arenas which stretch your comedy skills. Once people know who you are and come to see you specifically, there is a sense that the danger element has melted away. That's not to say that you don't have to make 'em laugh – you do – but there is the cushion of the audience always being fans.

On the whole, corporate event organisers tend not to tell their audience which entertainer they will see, until said entertainer is announced onto the stage. And I can tell you that on many occasions I have tripped onto the stage accompanied by an audible sigh of despair from the audience when they realise it is me and not Jimmy Carr/Jim Davidson/Michael McIntyre or whoever it was they wanted.

Over the years I have taken part in corporates as diverse as the Mother and Baby Awards (heavy security when I did it, as apparently the year before, a fight had broken out between two tables), the Heating and Ventilation Awards, the British Association of Air Conditioning Engineers and quite a few media/advertising awards.

Obviously, many of these awards or dinners contain an audience who are not my natural constituency and therefore I have had to work my proverbial bollocks off. It's a bit like starting at the bottom of a big black pit, looking up at the audience and trying to claw your way out.

At the Heating and Ventilation Awards, I was faced with an audience composed mainly of middle-aged men in suits. I had managed to get hold of a copy of their trade magazine, unsurprisingly called *Heating and Ventilation Monthly/Weekly* . . . whatever it was. They looked at me with suspicion as I came on. I started by waving a copy of the magazine at them and stated, 'This magazine is the bollocks!' It was a risky strategy which could have gone horribly wrong and I was lucky that it worked. A big laugh went round the room, thank God, and I was halfway up out of my deep, dark pit.

There have been many occasions when my strategy *hasn't* worked. I remember being in a hotel in Birmingham once with probably the most pissed group of people I have ever met, outside of the Comedy Store Friday-night late show, and I had been placed right in the middle of them with a slightly crap mic on a very low raised platform. There then followed half an hour of drunken abuse, which I attempted to parry as best I could with a few well-aimed put-downs, picking on the troublemakers like a teacher and using only the jokes which I knew normally stormed it. Eventually the whole affair just descended into mayhem, with people throwing bits of bread roll, shouting at me to get off and turning to chat to their mates. Oh, the humiliation.

Eventually I got off, roughly five minutes before my allotted time-slot, and escaped to my dressing room – which was akin to a broom cupboard halfway down a corridor – and contemplated the cheery three-hour drive home examining my failure.

Other very difficult corporate gigs tend to happen when you find yourself not only doing the stand-up bit at the beginning, but hosting the awards as well. This means that you are on stage for about two hours on average, and the more awards there are, the more likely it is that at some point the audience will lose the will to live. However much you throw at it, eventually they just want you to shut up – and I have every sympathy with that.

I once did an international TV awards ceremony at the Hammersmith Palais with Ruby Wax. There were 100 awards and we tried to steel ourselves for a long night. We thought at least we would be able to banter a bit with each other to keep it going. Rather disastrously, we discovered our mics had been set miles apart and the way the sound was organised meant that we couldn't hear what the other was saying. So we spent an excruciating three hours going 'Pardon?' a lot to each other and looking miserably at our scripts as the audience descended into a coma. Nightmare.

Perhaps one of the hardest awards I ever did was an advertising bonanza. It was on at the huge cavern-like room in the Grosvenor House Hotel, which used to be an ice-rink, and there were over 1,000 guests who, shall we say, all had a diploma in getting very drunk, very quickly.

I found myself taking the piss out of one particular company that just kept winning everything. It was very good-natured, there was a lot of banter and the audience seemed to be enjoying themselves. Finally we came to the last award of the evening, which was for Company of the Year – and sure enough, this company won again. Mayhem ensued.

I'm making all these corporate gigs sound like nightmares, but obviously the ones that went wrong are more interesting. On the whole they can be really enjoyable and give you a huge sense of satisfaction that you have fought and won a battle against a group of people who often seem determined not to like you.

## Awards Ceremonies

I tend not to go to awards ceremonies myself because I find them hard work. As someone who's pretty crap at looking smart, the red carpet's always a bit of an ordeal. I'm making it sound like I get invited to loads. I don't.

I do get asked to the British Comedy Awards, but that always looks like such a bunfight I'd rather watch it on the telly.

Awards ceremonies are, in short, a huge ordeal. First of all you have to run the gauntlet of paps on the way in, and there are the usual concerns such as, 'Have I got a bogey on show?' 'Are my pants going to fall down?' 'How am I going to stop myself hitting them?'

I went to the BAFTAs with Trinny and Susannah, and that was enough for me. Just the atmosphere of barely controlled hysteria on that one occasion was enough to last me a lifetime. And I didn't even have to sit through the bloody thing either. I was back stage having a laugh and still it seemed to drag on interminably.

I also think it's really hard for the judges to make a decision about who is the best because there are wildly different programmes and personalities in each category. How can you compare Harry Hill with *QI* with Ant and Dec? I wouldn't have a clue.

Of course, the main awards which come up for me are the comedy bits of telly awards and stand-up awards. I managed to get out of my first awards ceremony at the Glasgow Comedy Festival simply by not being there. Hattie Hayridge and I had done a stand-up show together and then gone back to London and so we weren't actually there when they announced the winners. We each received a little boat-shaped award in the post, and I gave mine to my mum. I was very pleased, but in a lot of ways I wonder what the awards really mean. I won't get all philosophical here; suffice to say I don't immediately reach for the bread-knife if I don't win things.

The Comedy Awards, which are held every year, are normally hosted by Jonathan Ross, and ever since some 'inappropriate' contributions by some of the performers in the past, the event now seems to be pre-recorded most of the time. Each one is subject to the moods, aided and abetted by a fair old sloshing of alcohol, of the comics present.

I won the award for Best Newcomer one year and an award for Best Stand-up another year. The awards are heavy glass-type things containing a joker from a pack of cards and would be perfect for knocking out a burglar, should the need ever arise. Because I didn't go to any of the ceremonies I was asked to record a little acceptance speech earlier so I knew I'd won something, but I have heard recently that some awards organisers, if they hear a performer isn't coming, give the award to someone else. So, at least I can convince myself that I have actually won and they've given it to someone else if I haven't turned up.

My highlights from the Comedy Awards over the years have been:

1. Sean Lock, who on receiving a Best Newcomer Award, gave a little speech which included the words . . . 'and I'd like to say hello to all my new friends.' Hugely cynical maybe, but very funny.

2. In 1993, Julian Clary declaring to Jonathan Ross that 'I've just been fisting Norman Lamont' back stage. Norman Lamont was a Tory politician and Chancellor of the Exchequer at the time. The punch line that followed was drowned out somewhat by the guffaws of laughter: 'Talk about a red box.'

The best thing was the shock and outrage of the right-wing tabloids the next day, who reported that there was shocked silence. That's strange, because everyone I spoke to who was there said the entire audience pissed themselves laughing.

# Charity Matters

Charity is big business these days and charities all seem to feel that they need a high-profile face attached to them in order to garner support and more importantly, dosh. Over the years, as my profile has risen, so have the requests for benefits, patronage, auction items, cartoons (can't draw to save my life), poems and TV appearances for big fundraisers such as Comic Relief. I do try to do as much as I can in terms of benefits because I think if you are in as fortunate a position as I am, you should do what you can for others who aren't.

There is, of course, the argument put forward by cynics that comedians only do big benefits to advance their careers – but then again, you wouldn't be asked to do big benefits unless you were fairly high-profile anyway.

On the comedy circuit in the eighties, many charities started to run benefits to publicise themselves and raise money. I did several benefits for Amnesty International, including one to raise money to fight against the imprisonment of two comedians in Myanmar (once Burma), just for making jokes about the military government. God, if you were thrown into prison in this country for taking the piss out of the government, we'd all be in there.

I think comics do have a part to play in raising awareness, and giving their time for these sorts of events.

Performing live at benefits is an odd thing. On many occasions, audiences have been slightly strange, giving the impression that they've paid their money and now they want to be entertained. It's hard to describe, but there is a slightly critical feeling in the air. Hence a lot of benefits have been rather subdued affairs. This is not to say loads of them haven't been great, but on a number of occasions I have found myself thinking, Bloody hell, I've come all the way up here and they don't even seem that pleased – but that is the childish resentful side of my personality that wants people to be grateful, and I apologise for that.

One charity I'm a patron of and of which I'm very fond is the Alzheimer's Society. I try to support charities which are slightly unfashionable, non-cuddly and not particularly attractive, a bit like me. The elderly in this country are a forgotten generation and let's face it, we're all going to get there at some point – me probably before most of you.

The elderly seem ever more vulnerable these days too, to what is called 'elder abuse', and so I have done the odd benefit, radio appeals and had my gob plastered over mail-outs. It takes such a relatively short amount of time so I can't understand why all performers and comics don't do it, although to be fair to them, the vast majority do.

The Donna Louise Trust runs a hospice for children outside Stoke. I have visited on a couple of occasions and three times have done a benefit at the Victoria Hall in Stoke. On these occasions, Nick Hancock, David Baddiel, Andy Robinson and I have done a show in which Andy compered, Nick interviewed Dave, and I finished the night off with stand-up. God, am I sounding 'holier than thou' enough yet? I don't mean to, but it is a risk even talking about charity, coming across like you think you're Mother Blinking Teresa. So I'll keep the altruistic trumpet-blowing to a minimum.

## Comic Relief

Comic Relief is a charity I've been involved with over the years. My initial contact with them was when I made a brief appearance on *Comic Relief* night in the early nineties, in a queue of people lining up to kiss Dawn French.

One fateful year when I must have been slightly pissed I agreed that I would run the London Marathon to raise money for Comic Relief. It wasn't as though I had decided that from a starting-point of no exercise at all, and would suddenly rise up off the settee and leg it for twenty-six miles. I had already been running for a bit, having been emotionally blackmailed into it by a couple of friends. We went to a group run by another friend who is a personal trainer. Having done no running whatsoever before and not exactly being in the tip-top bracket of fitness, I was a little worried that I'd run a few steps and drop dead. We started by running round some school playing-fields, and in order to kick it off without fatalities we were advised to walk twenty steps, run twenty, walk twenty, etc. Even that was a shock to my system and after a couple of minutes of doing that, I honestly thought my lungs were bleeding. For some reason though, I stuck at it and I did notice after several weeks that it was getting easier.

Finally, I was able to run without stopping which was a bit of an advance. As the weeks went on, we upped our running distances so that on occasion I did four or five miles at a time. And it was at this point that I was called by Comic Relief to ask if I could do the London Marathon. Foolishly, I agreed. There then ensued six months of training, which was bloody hard work. Each month I added on a few extra miles. The main problem was it took so bloody long. I'm sure you can imagine I'm not the fastest runner in the country, so each Sunday morning was allocated for a progressively longer run.

Eventually, with the Marathon looming, I managed to persuade my friend Sam to come and do a couple of long runs with me . . . round the perimeter of Richmond Park twice (a mere fifteen miles). God, it was fucking awful. We arrived on two occasions at seven o'clock in the morning in March (yes, bloody freezing) and parked the car in a car park from which we set off 'running' which was more, in my case, of a wheezing shuffle. Rather demoralisingly, the first mile or so was uphill and I felt ready to cave in after that. But run it we did after a fashion, even though it took about four hours. At the end of the first run I couldn't even feel my legs, which morphed into pillars of concrete. Also, on the way, a few people stopped me to say hello and have a chat. Those who stopped me during the last three miles or so probably got short shrift as I was fairly convinced by then that I would never walk again.

Anyway, having done the crippling fifteen miles twice, I was pretty sure that adding an extra eleven miles would, at the very least, result in my legs dropping off and wondered if I was ever going to make it. I was never to be tested, however, because about a week before the London Marathon I began to feel really grim in a sore-throaty, headachy, hurty-legs kind of way. I thought it would pass in a couple of days, but it didn't, so I shuffled along to the doc who told me I would be mad to try and run the Marathon. Secretly, I was relieved because I couldn't envisage making it round the whole course and it's SO public. I may have another bash in the future, but who knows?

Other Comic Relief projects have been slightly easier on my heart and lungs. When my second daughter was a few months old, I was asked to do *Fame Academy* for

Comic Relief. This was a programme in which various celebs had a singing competition and each day one of us was voted out by the public. It involved going and staying in a huge posh house in Highgate for the duration of the contest. I did not want to stay away from home so said I couldn't do it, but eventually was given a special dispensation to go home every day, which suited me as I'm not very good at that dormitory thing with people I don't know.

On the show were nine of us: Fearne Cotton, Kwame Kwei-Armah, Ulrika Jonsson, John Thomson, Paul Ross, Doon Mackichan, Ruby Wax, Will Mellor and me.

Before the show started we were asked which songs we wanted to do. I think we had to do about ten. Well, I thought to myself, it's a comedy show so let's go for it. I thought I'd do 'Psychokiller' by Talking Heads for starters and maybe a song from a kids' programme called *Bear in the Big Blue House* which my daughters loved. Sadly, I was prevented because there was a song-list we had to choose from, with a fair bit of middle-of-the-road stuff on it. So I picked Dusty Springfield among other things, although I knew I would cock it up big time. I think David and Carrie Grant, who were the singing teachers on the show, probably thought this too, but very kindly never mentioned it. I can hold a tune, but this is the limit of my performance skills as far as singing goes. I knew I'd get chucked out pretty sharpish.

I managed to get through the first and second night as Paul Ross and Fearne Cotton got flung out. On the third day we were talked through the procedure of booting someone out, the killer blow being that the celebs were narrowed down to two by a public vote and the other celebs had to decide which one went, by individually voting for them. We practised this and John Thomson and I were randomly allotted the parts of the guinea-pig chuckees. People filed up to vote and voted me out.

That night, it all went hideously wrong for me singing 'Build Me Up, Buttercup'. I couldn't hear the intro music over the noise of the crowd and put in a shockingly bad performance as well as being two bars of music behind. Predictably I was in the bottom two, and weirdly, so was John Thomson too. As the celebs filed up to choose between us I knew I would go, and when my name was announced I pretended to faint to give the others a laugh. John Thomson's face was a picture. I think he thought I'd really fainted.

Anyway, it was a bloody great relief to get back home. Also, I needed to be booted out that night as I had another job, which I had to start the next day, so it all worked out well.

A couple of years later, I did *The Apprentice You're Fired* for Comic Relief too. We were an interesting combo. The women's team consisted of Cheryl Cole, Trinny Woodall, Maureen Lipman, Karren Brady and me. The men's team was Rupert Everett, Danny Baker, Piers Morgan, Alastair Campbell and Ross Kemp.

We were shown into Sir Alan's 'boardroom' and in came the famous old grump himself and instructed us to raise as much money as possible; whoever did so would be the winner. I attempted to bribe the old curmudgeon with some chocolate, and although there was the ghost of a smile on his face, he played the part of old git to perfection.

Our task was to run an urban funfair with attractions and food in Central London. We had to bid against the men's team for certain stalls that we thought would raise the most money, and this farce was filmed as we didn't get the stalls we wanted, following a bit of Machiavellian manoeuvring by Piers and Alastair. Trinny pretty much took charge and started scaring people into giving her money right away under the guise of 'buying a ticket for the event', while Karren and Cheryl stayed in the hotel phoning people, either to get them to offer something as a raffle prize, or to make a guest appearance on the night, and offer some sort of service to someone who paid them loads of money. Not sex obviously, although I met a few dodgy, wealthy guys who I think would have been quite happy to pay for a quickie with a famous person.

We also needed to provide food stalls on the night so Maureen and I were despatched to a kitchen in Bermondsey to prepare the food. (Yes, the glamour of this didn't go unremarked by us, the older contingent.) We were faced with a mountain of preparation, but we had a right good laugh doing obscene things with squid and forgetting to put a big container of chicken away in the fridge, so it went off overnight.

On the night of the funfair things were looking good, the food was ready, stars were booked to wander round, and a load of rich people had bought tickets to attend. Maureen and I were dressed as clowns and stayed serving on the food stall. Many times, characters from the boys' team would run over and take the piss and inform us for the zillionth time that they were going to win. But I knew that our secret weapon – Trinny – had cornered a few, very wealthy old ladies and felt fairly confident.

During the filming we came into contact with some

of the country's richest people and ended up at a party at Matthew Freud's house where I saw David Cameron, Jerry Hall, Claudia Schiffer and lots of other, very well-heeled guests. I'm afraid I have a natural antipathy towards wealthy people, I just can't help it. I met Philip Green and Stuart Rose, both of whom run huge businesses, and I couldn't get away fast enough. They both seemed to have the attitude that because they were so wealthy, people would fall at their feet. I have nothing to say to such businessmen and I'm sure they have nothing to say to short fat middle-aged female comics either.

At one point Karren and I were leaning against the wall surveying all this wealth, unaware that she was leaning on a huge Gilbert and George original.

'Excuse me, can you get off my painting,' said a voice. There stood Gilbert . . . or George – I've no idea.

Suffice to say that the women's team won the fund-raising by hundreds of thousands of pounds. Girl power! I am being ironic here, since that particular call to action has done more to destroy true feminist principles than the combined work of John McCririck and Margaret Thatcher.

My most recent foray into Comic Relief-ness was being persuaded to dress up as Britney Spears and do a silly dance for *Let's Dance for Comic Relief*. I was given the choice of three performers to emulate, Kylie Minogue, Beyoncé and Britney Spears. It wasn't a difficult decision to make since, much as I recognise their talent, I prefer Britney out of the three. I feel sorry for Britters – she has had a rough ride from the press and struggles with maintaining a balance in the amoral, evil world that being a pop star can be. However, I liked the song, 'Hit Me Baby One More Time' although I thought the video pandered to the worst male, slightly paedophilic view some men hold of schoolgirls. Thus I felt it was ripe for a piss-take. I like dancing and I don't mind looking like a twat for charity.

I had roughly a week or so of training with a lovely woman called Steph who patiently repeated my steps for me in various dance studios in London. She was a good laugh, and we also had a good laugh doing it, which is very important. This was overseen by Richard, the boss of the teachers, and his well-placed raised eyebrow on occasions told me all I needed to know about my dancing skills.

Eventually I was ready to train with the other dancers, who put me to shame by learning the steps in what seemed to be about twenty seconds. I was slightly trepidatious of what they would think of me, as the svelte and (what had seemed to me) slightly haughty attitude of dancers wasn't really something that appealed to me. I needn't have worried; they were all friendly and helpful. I felt for the poor sods who had to pick me up at one point and move me from one part of the floor to another. When I actually put the costume on for the first time, I roared with laughter because I looked so bloody ridiculous, but it all added to the surrealism of the occasion that was looming.

So I had good fun – right up until the night of the show, when I realised just how uncomfortable my Britney Spears costume was going to be. Once sewn into it I couldn't have a wee, and if you are doing live telly, nerves dictate that you want to go to the lav approximately every twelve seconds. As I had two hours to wait until the show started, I seriously considered just letting myself go in the costume – not really an option for the poor dancers who had to lift me up though.

On the day, we did a camera rehearsal in the afternoon and then waited for the show itself to happen. It was hosted by Claudia Winkleman, a terrifying powerhouse of a woman who never seems to be below 11 on her energy clock. But she is up for a laugh, as is her co-host Steve Jones, and I had to be on my guard because it was a live show and I have a terrible tendency to shoot my mouth off and say rude things.

I had assumed, owing to my pretty poor Britney impersonation, that I would not get through the first round and had organised a weekend away with the family. When I got through to the final, having been picked by the judges as the third finalist I thought, Oh, I'm not going to be able to go away. We did, but I had to drive up from Canterbury on the day and was away for hours.

The final was good fun because as usual I had invested no energy in hoping I would win. Everyone knew it would be Robert Webb who had done a scarily accurate performance of 'What a Feeling' from the musical *Flashdance*. Paddy McGuinness and Keith Lemon also stood a good chance. I was there to enjoy myself and try to remain continent.

On the night, poor Lisa Maxwell from *The Bill* had a dodgy tummy so between us we were worried that the finale of the show might be a little more than people had bargained for.

As I predicted, the victory of Robert Webb was a foregone conclusion. But my daughters loved it and had a good laugh, and at least they thought I should have won.

## Power-boat Hell

Occasionally you offer to do something for charity and when you get there, you wonder if you were completely insane to agree to it. One such event was a power-boat racing day down in Portsmouth which I had been asked to do by Jeremy Clarkson's wife, Francie. Jeremy Clarkson and I do not see eye to eye on a huge number of areas and I find myself occasionally referring to him in my stand-up as shorthand for someone who is a Little Englander and who jealously seems to guard the 'British' way of life and is constantly having a pop at other European nations. As someone who is acutely aware to some extent of how it feels to be an outsider through working in mental health, having German family and being in comedy, I find this very unpalatable.

This is not, however, the reason to date that I have not bombed round the circuit in 'a reasonably priced car' on *Top Gear*. The main thing stopping me is that, having had two brothers, I am enormously competitive, and fear that if I ever stepped into that aforementioned vehicle, I would probably kill myself in the process. So I have declined so far, but am sure I will be tempted soon. Jeremy Clarkson is unfailingly polite and friendly in real life, and I cannot fault him socially. He and his mates on *Top Gear* love a bit of risk, as was evidenced by Richard Hammond's spectacular stunt in a cart-wheeling car on *Top Gear* a while ago. And this day was no exception.

One of the reasons I'd said I would do this event was because my friend Jayne, who sorts out all my charity requests and fanmail for me, has a son who is a huge fan of the show, so I went down there with him and her to give him an opportunity to have a look at the stars in person.

The point of the day was to raise money for a children's hospice called Helen and Douglas House, and the way this was achieved was to get big companies to sponsor a power-boat which would take part in races round the harbour. Each company had sent a couple of gung-ho young men who were to have a crack at driving a boat. In order to attract them, a bevy of celebs had been invited and each boat had two blokes, an instructor and a celebrity in it. Other celebs attending that day that I can remember were Jimmy Carr, Brian Conley and Jane Moore, who is a well-known *Sun* columnist.

Many photos were taken and then eventually we climbed aboard a power-boat. The two men were very excited, one more than the other, and he asked if he could go first. We all concurred and he got into the driving seat. The sea seemed slightly choppy and I began to wonder when my breakfast would reappear.

Our instructor was a very sweet, mild-mannered woman and she gave us a quick run-through: some instructions emphasising the safety aspects, then it was time to set off.

Our slightly over-keen driver had obviously decided to go for it big-time, and before we knew it, he had floored the accelerator and we set off at a terrifying speed which threw us all back in our seats. Our instructor looked a bit perturbed by this burst of enthusiasm and warned against further acceleration. But our intrepid driver was away with the fairies, her voice was very quiet and he chose either not to hear her, or ignored her. His companion, who was in the seat beside me, looked positively green. The boat at one point tipped dangerously to one side and my elbow grazed the water. We all had life-jackets on and I began to visualise falling out and banging my head on the boat as I went, then sinking to the bottom of Portsmouth Harbour. We then looked as if we were going to do a somersault and my companion turned to me and shouted, 'We're all going to die!' At that point he and I joined in with the instructor and shouted various helpful technical suggestions like, 'For fuck's sake, slow down!'

It sort of worked and he did a bit. By that time, thank the Lord, his 'go' was over and he slowed the boat to a halt and jumped out of the seat, declaring, 'That was brilliant!' and let his companion into the driving seat. The latter drove like a Sunday school teacher on major tranquillisers, as did I when I got my opportunity. I think we came last but I didn't give a toss about that, I was just glad not to have drowned.

When we arrived on shore again, I discovered that all the celebs who had kids had felt similarly to me and had seen their lives flash before their eyes, whereas the young, single and carefree types like Jimmy Carr announced it to be one of the best days of their lives.

So, my involvement with charity events has led to snogging, singing, sailing, running, dancing and kicking the arses of some quite annoying blokes. It's been bloody brilliant.

# (Not) Doing Ads

Over the years I have been offered the opportunity to front some advertising campaigns, either in person or as a voiceover. I can't imagine what on earth I've got that might persuade people to buy a product, but who knows how the minds of advertising execs work? At the risk of sounding 'holier than thou' there are many reasons why I will never do ads.

First of all, the words of George Orwell, the Über-leftie author of *1984* and *Animal Farm*, often resound in my head. He said that advertising is 'the rattling of a stick inside a swill bucket' and I can't help but agree with him.

Our system needs to advertise things to sell them

(obviously) and if there is not a market for certain products, they will create one. For example, many products have appeared on the market recently, aimed at very specific age groups of children, and once some products are spotted by children because of ads, a huge demand is created. Even worse, children feel that they are not a fully paid-up member of their peer group unless they own that particular product. I don't like this. It puts pressure on parents and kids and is not fair.

Also, many electronic products now have built-in obsolescence so that they have to be replaced every few years, and advertisers have to make it sound as if you're getting something new for your money, when in fact your old whatever-it-is would probably do just as well. The world of fashion is a really good case in point. Each season a whole new raft of clothes appears on the catwalks, some of them utterly bloody ridiculous, but some stupid arses go ahead and buy them because they think they must – although I have to admit I have never seen anyone wearing any of the more wacky designs that make them look like a bush on legs or a zombie with liver disease.

One of the other main reasons I don't do ads is because once you spout support of a company for money, they sort of own you, and should you ever have occasion to slag them off, or any of their products, you simply cannot do this. I know it is a small thing, but to me as a comic, it's very important not to be owned by anyone and to be able to say what I like when I like and wherever I like.

Having said all this, I wouldn't criticise people who do choose to do ads, because that's up to them as an individual – and it's hardly killing your grandmother, is it? Perhaps those who said they would never do ads and then did them are slightly more culpable, and I find it completely puzzling that some comics would slag off others for doing an ad when they themselves do advertising voiceovers. Is it any different if people can't see your face?

I don't think so.

If you find my little sermon dull, please have a look on youtube.com at Bill Hicks's rant about advertising. He puts it much better than I could.

# Festival Shenanigans

One of the times I would love to be invisible is at festivals. There's nothing I like better than to wander round just drinking in the fantastic atmosphere, looking at the bonkers stalls and lying in a tent listening to snoring, giggling, shouting, laughing, singing and the general festival hubbub.

I went to Glastonbury a couple of times in the eighties, one time boiling hot and full of pissed pink people and the other time absolutely swamped in mud, but very manageable if you're off your face.

Since then I have performed at Glastonbury, Reading and Latitude (apparently nicknamed 'Latte-tude' because it is *so* middle class).

I think the secret, if you stay overnight at festivals, as you know you're not going to get a decent night's sleep, is to self-medicate, which I normally do with alcohol. Although you feel shit in the morning, at least unconsciousness has been much easier to achieve. Glastonbury is the only festival I've actually stayed at, however; all the others I've either come home from or have gone straight on to somewhere else afterwards.

Reading always happens in the middle of the Edinburgh Festival so that's the closest I've ever got to feeling like a mega-star: being flown down to Reading and then back up the same day to continue doing my shows. I suppose if you are on the road a lot you get used to things like a bed, a kettle and a telly, and these days, a hangover lasts a hell of a lot longer than it used to when I was a sprightly young thing in my thirties.

When people clock you, it's a totally different experience at a festival. At Latitude I felt like the Pied Piper because when I went for a wander I was followed round by autograph-hunting children and eventually had to give up and go and hide. My experience of Reading made me think that they could just as well put a cardboard cut-out on stage as the heaving, sweaty, delirious audience don't really seem to care what's on stage. And good luck to 'em, that's what music festivals are for.

Literary festivals like Hay and Cheltenham are a different kettle of fish altogether. More subdued and with an older, middle-class punter, they are altogether a more genteel affair. The green room at Hay is a veritable cornucopia of literary bedazzlement. It seems so weird to sit amidst Jeremy Paxman, Alan Bennett, Gore Vidal and Terry Jones. I tend to promote books at literary festivals and of course the stakes aren't as high as they are with stand-up so it's a real pleasure because I don't get the usual accompanying butterflies.

Again, I tend not to stay at Hay as my mum lives quite near by, so I go to her place and she comes with me to whatever sort of show I'm doing. At the moment I alternate every year between doing a Q and A about my latest book and performing stand-up. It's quite strange having your own mum in the audience and I suppose to some extent it could be quite limiting. But I have to keep remembering that my mum is in her seventies and I am in my fifties and she won't get up and tell me I'm not allowed out for a week if I swear.

# Pretending To Be a
# Rally Driver

I love driving, and during one tour with my tour manager John, after one particularly long and hair-raising journey from Devon across to Surrey when we were late and John did rather too much driving in the middle of the road to get us there in time, we mooted the idea of having a crack at rally driving. On our travels, we had met a lovely guy called Gary whose son worked at a rally school so we arranged to go down there and have a go.

It was really exciting being given permission to put your foot down on a muddy track that wound round sharp corners and up over bumps, and I was bitten by the bug almost immediately.

Things moved on apace and we found ourselves with our own rally car (a used Peugeot, cheap and little). I had also managed to get Channel Four to agree to us making a documentary about getting my international licence which would lead up to the Rally of Great Britain.

We tried a few rally race days and I suppose we were unusual, because we both wanted to have a go at the driving, rather than one of us always being the navigator and the other always driving. Navigating is a stressful job in a different way; you have a very detailed set of instructions in front of you describing the exact layout of the course. Bends are divided into different categories so that in theory you can tell your driving partner how much he has to slow down, but we weren't very good at it and much of the time whoever was navigating was slightly behind the driver and would shout out, 'Sharp bend coming up!' just as we were going round it, or veering off the road.

Our first rally was on a race-track down in Sussex. By this time we had been kitted out in rally-driving suits which I have to tell you are not the most flattering outfits even if you look like a twig, which I don't;

you feel as if you are in your own personal sauna. Add to this a helmet with an inbuilt microphone 'cause you can't hear a bloody thing once the helmet's on and the total effect is claustrophobic. And that's *before* you even get in the bleeding car.

Once you're in the car, it gets worse. You are strapped in with a four-way seat belt and surrounded by the internal cage-like structure of the car, which is designed to stop you being killed if the car rolls. Quite useful, then.

However, it does mean you feel trapped once you're in there; your movements are severely restricted and if you want to go for a piss, forget it. As a woman you have to peel the whole bloody thing down to your ankles. Once, however, I was so desperate, I legged it off into the woods at the start of a rally, took a quick look round to make sure I was alone, did the business and then as I was hauling it all up, realised I was being observed from some distance away by a large group of spectators – there to watch the rally, not me having a wee.

One very special feature of the rallies that we took part in was an excess of mooning. Word had gone out at some of the rallies that I was competing and on more than one occasion I would round a corner, concentrating like mad, to be presented with a delightful bare white arse that obviously hadn't seen the sun since its nappy was left off. Once there was even a row of about five. This brightened up my rallies and I almost began to expect it after a while.

It has to be said that John and I were pretty shit rally drivers and even worse navigators. Although we enjoyed it, we were glorious amateurs really, and nowhere near the class of the professionals. As the training rallies went on, we started to get a better feel for it, although we got lost quite a lot and grew used to driving up to ramblers and walkers and asking, 'Have you seen a lot of rally cars go past?' If they hadn't we knew we were well off-piste.

At one rally in which I was navigating we drove off the start ramp and as I hadn't really been concentrating on the cars that went before us, I said to turn left – whereas they had all apparently turned right. We found ourselves down a cul de sac after five minutes and had to go back to the start so I could follow the map again.

Our final rally before commencing the Rally of Great Britain was in Wales, and the start was very high up, nearly in the mountains. The run-up to the start was absolutely terrifying and ran alongside a sheer drop of hundreds of feet. Although we were only doing about three miles an hour I experienced something approaching a panic attack – not terribly impressive before the race had even begun!

Things went from bad to worse . . . we nearly crashed on a hairpin bend above a huge drop, and by the time we got to the end of the stage I staggered out of the car and vowed that I would never get in a rally car again. This somewhat messed up the whole point of our documentary, but we carried on with John agreeing to drive it, and taking on a new navigator; I, meanwhile, in a girly way, waited at the end of stages, interviewing spectators and drivers.

In fact, I interviewed the very talented driver, Richard Burns who sadly died far too young of a brain tumour. He informed me that women were rubbish rally drivers because they had no bollocks. In my case, he was absolutely correct – physically *and* metaphorically.

# Briefly in the Police

Rather bizarrely, in 2008 I was asked whether I would like to perform in the Gilbert and Sullivan operetta, *The Pirates of Penzance*, in a West End theatre.

Gilbert and Sullivan are quite old-fashioned in the sense that people who like them tend to be about 140 years old. But one of those people is my dad, who used to play quite a lot of the stuff when I was a child so I had many of the tunes in my head. Also, I thought it might give him an opportunity to actually come to something he might enjoy rather than pretending to.

The company who wanted to put the show on were called Carl Rosa; they perform exclusively Gilbert and Sullivan operettas and they thought that if they bunged a few so-called celebs into the mix, it might open G&S up to a whole new audience.

*The Pirates of Penzance* is a reasonably straightforward tale of love and intrigue. I was asked to play the part of the Police Sergeant, which had never been played by a woman before. The role suited me as my voice is quite low and I am elderly, so I would hardly be in line to play the heroine Mabel, who wears nice dresses and warbles up to unfeasibly high notes. Also, not much is called for on the acting front: a fair bit of striding about, barking orders and looking strict. I also thought it might be a nice opportunity to wear a Victorian policewoman's costume. Not that there was such a thing, because in Victorian times, policewomen did not exist.

The last and only time I had worn a policewoman's costume was for a sketch show, and I found myself wearing a costume with the name *Joan Sims* sewn into it. Joan was, of course, a luminary of the *Carry On* films and I felt like I was wearing comedy history.

To get in some practice, I wandered out on the street for a bit and pretended to be a proper policewoman. I told a few people off for parking offences, and it was amazing to discover how much deference people have towards the police.

In order to start the process off, I had to learn the

songs . . . two of them: 'When the Foeman Bares His Steel' (yes, I'm none the wiser, sounds a bit pervy though, doesn't it?), and 'The Policeman's Song', a well-known ditty that most people have heard at one time or another. I went to a studio in Central London where a lovely man called Duncan put me through my paces. I don't have a good voice but managed to growl along to it on the lower register. He gave me the OK and said he thought it was unlikely people would throw things as soon as I opened my mouth.

It was then on to rehearsals in a room down the road. I found the whole thing daunting as all the other performers were regular G&S aficionados. Still, I had to bite the bullet and be prepared to look like a twat in front of them. So I jumped in with both feet.

I had my own little gang of policemen, bless 'em, hardly a heterosexual among them, and when we first practised our march onto the stage, the choreographer Steve said something like, 'For fuck's sake, you're supposed to be marching, not carrying baskets of flowers.'

It was such a good laugh and I could have just done rehearsals for ever, but in what seemed like a very short time, round came the actual show at the Apollo in Shaftesbury Avenue. I had already been to see *The*

*Mikado* which starred Alistair McGowan, who was so good in it that I began to worry I would cock things up really badly. I tried not to do that comparing thing, because down that road lurks depression. There is always going to be someone better than you.

On the first night I was all but paralysed with fear, terrified that a tiny squeak would come out of my mouth, followed by me running off stage, simultan-eously wetting myself and crying. I must have gone to the lav seven or eight times in the last ten minutes, and then I was pushed towards back stage, given my truncheon . . . and then I heard the opening notes to our march and suddenly I was on the stage waving my truncheon like a good 'un and doing an approximation of singing.

For the first few nights I hit a note an octave above what I was supposed to be singing and I could see the appealingly strict conductor Richard looking at me like I was mental. It hardly seemed to matter though and we comedied it up as much as possible before marching off to laughs and applause. I then had quite a bit of time to go out through the stage door and have a fag before I was back on to do 'The Policeman's Song' and deliver the few lines I had.

There is a big closing number and I was dressed up

in some sort of wedding dress for a laugh and had to enter under a garland of flowers with Bev, who played Ruth. We spent the time waiting to go on chatting about a number of varied subjects, and during one particularly interesting discussion about the menopause, missed our cue completely and had to run on at a pace slightly too demanding for two middle-aged ladies.

I did the show for two weeks and managed to get away with it. On one occasion I was slightly stressed out as I had to get to the Saturday matinée and had not realised what the time was. Glancing up at the clock I saw I was late, got my stuff together and ran out to the car. I slung open the boot, threw a bag in and bent down to check it was properly in. At this point the boot sprang back unexpectedly and whacked me on the top of the head. It hurt like hell and blood started gushing from the wound. Shit, what to do? Casualty? Lie down? Ignore it?

I went back in the house, got an enormous wodge of kitchen towel, bunched it up and held it on top of my head. I then drove up to the West End with one hand, using the other to keep the blood-soaked wodge of kitchen towel on my head. When I arrived, I had the mother of all headaches, but at least it seemed to have stopped bleeding, and as far as I could see, none of my brains were coming out. The make-up lady very delicately positioned my wig and helmet on top of a fresh wodge and onto the stage I sauntered, feeling like shit.

I got through the show, thanks to the help of the so-called Dr Footlights, a way I think to describe the rush of adrenalin which means that performers have been able to get through shows with illness, mega-hangovers or bits falling off, but I would not like to repeat the experience.

My dad did come to see the show and enjoyed it, so that was another ambition ticked off my list. And it felt great, being on the right side of the law for a change.

# Skipping Through the Bluebells

Although I probably look like I am well at home in my townie skin, I do actually love being out in the countryside. I make regular trips up to Shropshire and revel in wearing scruffy old wellies and wandering round listening to the birds singing.

This is why I was so pleased when, some years back, *Countryfile* with the iconic John Craven asked me to judge their photo competition for Children In Need. It takes two days a year and the initial day is to film a piece to go into the show, to give people the information they need to enter. Consequently, we tend to go somewhere country-ish but near enough to London so we can all get back in a day.

Once we have made the initial film telling the viewers the rules of the competition, then John, Chris Packham, the nature photographer and TV presenter, and I get together somewhere in a posh room full of photos and spend the day pulling out the best ones. By the end of the day, we have chosen the twelve that will go in the 'Children In Need' calendar. It is an absolutely marvellous day. Chris Packham is such a nice bloke and a good laugh, and we enjoy rooting through the huge piles of pictures to pick the winners.

*Countryfile* pursuits have taken me to Ashdown Forest in East Sussex, to Barnes Wetland Centre in South-West London, and to various animal sanctuaries in Kent and Sussex. I have been eyed up by deer, chased by otters and lain on my tummy in the mud trying to get an imaginative picture of a sheep . . . harder than it sounds.

Once, whilst at the British Wildlife Centre down in East Surrey, we held our breath as a tiny duckling struck out across the pond in the otter compound where the mother duck had inadvisedly laid her eggs. As the duckling paddled merrily along, one of the otters slid noiselessly into the water looking for a pre-lunchtime duckling hors d'oeuvre. Seeing this, I all but waded in to try and scoop up the poor little bugger. Chris, on the other hand, is far more pragmatic than me and told me I had to get used to the idea. However, for once cuteness triumphed and our little hero managed to cross the pond and survived to fight another day. I don't know for how long, but at least I didn't have to witness the food chain in action.

The photos we judge can be absolutely stunning, and thankfully, Chris Packham is quite good at spotting fakes, because I don't have a clue. We also see lots of pictures of donkeys with hats on, groups of people with dogs, and very occasionally hysterically inappropriate ones – a car, a shop. Who knows what these people were thinking? My favourite over the years has to be the one of a caterpillar on a branch – a very unusual critter because it was white with a red stripe through it. The name should have been a clue – *Colgatus* . . . yes, it was toothpaste.

# Comedy Holidays with Comedy People

In the days when I had very few responsibilities, I spent several New Year weeks on holidays round Britain with a bunch of other comedians and assorted friends. Considering we were a pretty disorganised lot it was a bleeding miracle that we actually got it together really.

Our first holiday was in a rented cottage in Wells-Next-the-Sea in Norfolk, and there was a group of about ten of us. We walked, went on boat trips to see seals, walked to the pub, cooked huge communal meals, played games, drank vast quantities, argued, took the piss out of each other and generally had a laugh. And always, every year, a couple of poor sods had to drive back to London to fulfil the requirement of comedy clubs for comics to be tortured by an audience on New Year's Eve.

We always played lots of stupid games. Our favourite game at the time was 'the water game' which is very good, evil fun. You all sit round in a big circle, pick a category like British Birds and fill a glass half full with water. Then someone is designated to hold the glass of water and pick a British bird which they write down on a piece of paper to avoid accusations of cheating. Then you go round the circle of people one by one and everyone has to say a British bird. When somebody says the name of the bird that the water-holder has written down, the water is duly chucked in their face. Simple but effective, and the drunker you are the better.

On these holidays the core group consisted of: Bill Bailey and his girlfriend Kris, Alan Davies, Jim Miller, Jeff Green, Mark Lamarr, Andy Linden, Keith Dover and my friends Waggly and Jez. Other comics and girlfriends/boyfriends drifted in and out of the mix.

Bill Bailey, as you would imagine, is an absolute delight. Gentle, warm and easygoing, he is the perfect house-guest, because he is happy to do anything. He is a huge animal lover and a musical genius, so can be relied upon to provide musical accompaniment to any pissed singsong and is one of those people, like Jools Holland, who can pretty much play any request you care to throw at him. Considering my musical repertoire extends only to 'Chopsticks', 'Love Story', which I learned when I was fourteen, and that hideous Celine Dion song from *Titanic* which I learned for a joke, I am unsurprisingly rarely asked to take a seat at the piano.

Bill has a problem similar to mine, which is an inability to say no to requests for benefits. Consequently, I think he works far too hard – but any attempt on my part to persuade him to slow down would be a bit of pot and kettle.

Alan Davies is a good friend with whom I have had some massive laughs over the years. He is loyal, fun and very amusing. He is also good at arguing and I love a good argument, but one can guarantee that it will never get out of hand or be antagonistic. We have similar political views too and have never fallen out over anything.

His only flaw is that he is an Arsenal fan, but perhaps

I am just jealous because they have a much nicer ground than Crystal Palace, the team I support.

The year after Norfolk we went to Cornwall and stayed in a fantastic house overlooking the sea in St Mawes. Again there was just a huge amount of being very lazy after staying up all night playing games and drinking.

Several people waded into the sea in the dead of night because they were too pissed to realise it was foolish, and everyone else thought it was too entertaining an idea to warrant trying to stop them. Nobody drowned, I am pleased to report.

We went back to Norfolk again the following year and stayed near Diss. This was a slightly bad-tempered holiday and I seem to remember some allegations of people not pulling their weight domestically, but again, most of it passed in a haze of laughing and hangovers.

A brutal round of the water game also produced some retribution, with my friend Waggly chucking her water at the wrong person, because I had actually said the same thing she'd picked (Mother's Pride, since you ask – yes, we were doing bread) and then chucking it over Jeff Green who had picked an obscure make of bread from his home town in Cheshire which she couldn't possibly have heard of. Dear old Waggly didn't want to chuck it over me in case I was upset!

There was also an incident in a hotel pool where Waggly got into trouble in the deep end and very quietly attempted to sink to the bottom. Thank God, she was spotted by two blokes who immediately dived in and dragged her out. I apparently was sitting on the side of the pool and didn't even notice. It all happened so quickly. The first thing I saw was her being hauled out of the pool. So much for all those life-saving lessons at school when you had to wear your pyjamas. I just didn't have time to run up to my room and put them on.

We went on long walks and also went bowling, which I hate for some reason. I can't see the skill or enjoyment in chucking a heavy ball down a runway. So I would sit there slightly bored just waiting for people to finish so we could go home.

Our final holiday was in Devon near Chulmleigh, pronounced Chumley. We'd moved from a communal house by this time to a set of cottages laid out round a courtyard. One of our party met and romanced a cheese dealer, which meant that the fridge was constantly full up with bloody massive bits of cheese, and we spent New Year in the village carousing with the locals and being generally badly behaved.

After this, people seemed to drift apart a bit and no one got it together to organise another jaunt, but they were good fun while they lasted.

# My Family

My mum and dad are still going strong. My mum's now seventy-five and my dad is eighty. They don't live together any more, though they never got divorced, but live about ten miles away from each other, and keep in touch regularly.

On the whole they have had good health, although after having a stroke in his late fifties my dad all but retired from work.

My mum, on the other hand, finds it almost impossible to stop working since her retirement. Having been a very senior social worker in the field of child protection, she is frequently called upon to give advice, sit on boards, tribunals and the like.

Some years ago she had a minor heart attack and, true to form, didn't tell us, her children, until she had come out of hospital. To say she doesn't like to make a fuss is an understatement. I went up to see her afterwards and had a terrible scare. I was in the kitchen downstairs and went up to the sitting room on the first floor to find her lying on the floor on her tummy. My own heart skipped a beat and I rushed into the room, only to find she was attempting to programme the video.

Similarly, it used to worry me if I called her and she didn't pick up. One evening about nine I called and got no answer, although I knew that she should have been at home. I ended up phoning her neighbour and good friend, John, and persuading him to go and check she was OK as he had a key. Actually, Mum had gone to bed early because she was tired, and was alarmed when she heard a man's voice calling up the stairs in the dark. She said she thought it was the spirits come to get her!

My brothers are both happily ensconced in their domestic lives. My brother Bill lives down in Sussex and has four children in their twenties and a five year old, which I think is pretty hard work.

Every year, round about the time of Bill's birthday,

he brings about fifteen friends to a Palace match and we have a nice nosh-up and sit in the directors' box to watch the game.

I have been a Palace supporter since the seventies, when I trained as a nurse near the ground and we used to go in a big group and watch every home game. I loved standing on the terraces and listening to the banter in the crowd. The language was absolutely appalling on occasions but not just for the sake of it; there were genuine comedians in the crowd. There was never an air of threat and it was just a good laugh.

I very rarely heard any racism on the terraces, which cheered me up because that is one thing I cannot abide or understand.

I have to say I was very disappointed once in the early eighties when I went for a curry in a local Indian restaurant to discover a handful of Palace players behaving in a racist way towards the waiter. I couldn't keep my mouth shut and went up to the table and called them a bunch of wankers. Hardly, 'I have a dream,' but I just wanted to make a point. I then beat a hasty retreat as I suspected they wouldn't punch my lights out, but the lights of the male friends I was with.

Palace has had a chequered history of management over the years. He may not be everyone's cup of tea, but I always had a sneaking admiration for Terry Venables, who I've met on a number of occasions and who seemed like good fun. I've got to know the staff at the club pretty well and it's good to see the same faces when I go to a match. Much piss-taking goes on.

I don't often go to away games. I once went to QPR and it was well scary. There was a surging, rather pissed, large crowd and at one point I got carried along by them with my feet off the ground and couldn't do a bloody thing about it. It put me off going to away games and made me realise how easy it was for tragedies like Heysel to happen . . . terrifying.

Palace to me is a very lovable team. They're not particularly glamorous, and their brief sojourns in the Premier League have always had a skin-of-their-teeth, temporary feel to them. These days, I go when I can and enjoy it immensely and have happy memories of many games. Weirdly, I have never seen Palace lose a match that I was at, only win or draw. I'd like to keep it that way. (That's not to say that they don't lose – they lose all the time; I just don't go that often!)

Having said that Palace aren't a particularly successful, glamorous team, I used to think the England team were the bee's knees and now I just feel depressed when I think about them. I was so looking forward to the 2010 World Cup and fell for all the bullshit of the football pundits who said that we were in with a chance. The dire first game against the USA I put down to first-night nerves and let it pass. But then when the next two games proved to be of a similar standard, I wondered what was going on.

I tried to blame the manager for a bit but in the end it came down to the players, who seemed to have no skill and, more importantly, no enthusiasm. Our great hero Wayne Rooney seemed like someone else, i.e. me, trying to play football. Then the game against Germany happened and the last tiny drop of optimism dribbled out of me. Maybe we just have to accept we ain't as world class as we think we are, lower our sights and accept that qualifying is enough.

However, I did enjoy the French team's meltdown as I'm sure did the entire Irish nation, who were kept out of qualifying for the World Cup by Thierry Henry's gobsmacking bit of cheating.

Matt, my other brother, who lives in Germany, works in computers and is married with one son. He has had a rough couple of years. It all started when he and another man tried to lift a guy in an electric wheelchair onto a bus that did not have a raise-able platform. As Matt strained, he felt a huge crack in his spine and fell to the ground in pain – at which point the kindly bus driver just drove off.

Matt had broken his back. The one piece of luck was that the break was outwards, and therefore thank God he wasn't paralysed. However, he pretty much had to lie on his back for six months and was driven completely bonkers by this, as you would be.

Some two weeks after he was finally up and about, he took his dog for a walk in the woods and a rather lary big dog went for it. So he picked his dog up and the lary dog attacked *him* instead. He began to fall to the ground and could not put his hand out to break his fall because he was holding the dog. Result: broken collar bone.

Remaining faithful to the rule of three, he subsequently slipped over in the bath and broke his wrist when he hit the edge of the bath. Thankfully, Matt was not had any accidents since, but I suppose he is the epitome of accident-prone.

# My New Family

I met Bernie, who is now my husband, in the middle of the nineties, through a mutual friend at the Edinburgh Festival. He is a psychiatric nurse, and so from the kick-off we had plenty in common and had many long discussions about our work that no one else would have understood or been interested in. At the time, Bernie was working as a Community Psychiatric Nurse, which meant he went out of the hospital where he was based to visit people at home. This was the way that psychiatric services had been proceeding since the mid-eighties, the result of a move to gradually empty the big Victorian redbrick psychiatric hospitals in which those with mental-health problems had been separated from the rest of us.

I'm sure I have said somewhere else that, although I think the ethos behind this admirable idea was sound, the fact remains that, especially in big towns and cities, there isn't much of a community to speak of, thus many people have become isolated in their own homes with little support from their neighbours. Big cities are full of people who are slightly wary of one another and not quite as friendly as those in smaller communities, and most of us continue to remain suspicious of those who have had mental-health problems.

Bernie and I immediately clicked. He is a good laugh, which is obviously very important to me, and our attitudes to most other important things are pretty similar. Back in London we began to see each other on a regular basis and a year or so down the line he asked me to marry him.

I agreed (obviously), and we got married in Ludlow in 1997 in a small church with a handful of friends. We deliberately kept it quiet, because I did not want to face the prospect of even one uninvited photographer being present. My friends joined in the conspiracy with their usual enthusiasm. In fact, good old Waggly, who was staying at a local hotel and was hyper-aware of not giving the game away, when asked by the cab driver where she was going, initially said, 'I'm not telling you.' After he told her that would make things slightly difficult for him, she capitulated and gave him the address of the church.

My friend Griffo went to the flower shop to get the flowers for the church, and when the shop assistant politely enquired who was getting married, she panicked and said, 'I am.' There then followed a rush of congratulations and questions about where it was. Of course she couldn't remember the name of the bloody church and backed out of the place clutching her flowers trying not to look like she was completely mad.

We actually used her tiny little Italian car as the wedding car. True to form, the lovely Griffo hadn't cleared it out, and as I got in I crunched on a carpet of empty crisp packets and chocolate wrappers. The service was conducted by a friend of my mum's, a woman priest, and it was her first-ever wedding, so the local vicar stood in the background making sure she didn't cock it up.

My dad also came up with the comedy goods when,

outside the church he asked me, 'Who's that bloke coming up the path now?'

'Only my husband-to-be, Dad,' I replied. (Yes, he had met Bernie on numerous occasions.) It was a lovely cheery service. The organist, who also doubled as the local TV aerial fixer and was famous for scaling roofs in his bare feet, turned up in the nick of time from a job with a pair of jeans and trainers very visible under his surplice.

Although we were relatively few, when it came to the hymns luckily we had my lovely Grandma Maisie and my Aunt Paddy who between them could up the volume to eleven and even managed to drown out the obligatory crying toddler in the background.

For the first year or so we lived up in Shropshire in a small cottage in the middle of nowhere, but not far from the many relatives I had up there. However, it proved pretty difficult to conduct my work-life from there because of the travel aspect. It meant every piece of TV or radio I did would inevitably be in London, and therefore I was up and down like a yoyo, doing a huge amount of driving. Touring was different, because in theory, as you are going all over the country, you can start from anywhere you like so that was do-able.

I had always wanted to have children, although it

was not a completely easy ride initially. I had thought there might be some problems because of my age, so when I discovered I was pregnant I was delighted. We arranged a couple of weeks' hence to go and have an early scan at a local hospital and I was looking forward to seeing the little picture on the screen.

We arrived, were shown into a room and the doctor began scanning. His facial expression turned from benign to worried-looking fairly quickly, and he informed me that he was very sorry but, as he put it, 'There's nothing there.' This is called a blighted ovum.

I was absolutely astonished and shocked as I had not factored this possibility into my vision of the future at all. We went home feeling stunned, even though the doctor had tried to put a positive spin on it by saying something like, 'Well, at least we know you can get pregnant.'

He was absolutely right, it didn't take long before I did get pregnant again and I was so relieved. Things went fine until about the eleventh week, when one night while I was at home, I started to feel a bit unwell and crampy. I won't go into the gory details but it all went wrong again, and although not physically unbearable I felt really helpless and wondered if my two chances had passed. We both felt grim.

And then one day a few weeks later as I was driving off to a gig, I listened to a radio phone-in about pregnancy and miscarriage, and a guy phoned in to say his wife had had ten miscarriages in a row and still managed to give birth to three children. I felt more hopeful again.

So when I got pregnant a third time I tried to be positive. Things went along well, although I was told that because of my age I had a one in twenty-seven chance of giving birth to a baby with Down's syndrome. However, tests are increasingly sophisticated and with each trip for a scan my odds improved tenfold. We decided that given that our nearest hospital was a forty-five-minute drive away and I was what they flatteringly call an 'elderly prima gravida' (i.e. a first-time mother over the age of thirty-five), that we would move back to London, so we could be more like a five-minute drive away from our local services.

We found a house in South London and moved back. I had quite a nice time being pregnant, never felt sick let alone threw up, although I was more tired than I have ever been for the first few months. Obviously, there were some concerns medically because I was in my forties, but everything went as smoothly as it could.

I also had a tour arranged which coincided with the

seventh and eighth month of my pregnancy, which I was a bit worried about, plus we lost our tour manager John just before it began. So Bernie came on tour with me and it all went fine until the last gig. We arrived at a theatre which had the weirdest stage I had ever seen. It had a fairly steep sloping wooden floor covering the whole stage which they had made for their Christmas show, and my performance area was a small cut-out piece about three feet square. I was expected to somehow edge my way across this incline and jump into the little box to perform and repeat the process on the way back. Up until this point I had kept the pregnancy secret and didn't want that to change, although I was a bit anxious I would lose my footing and roll onto the front row who were incredibly close to the stage, injuring me and them.

After a very heated argument, there was no alternative but to go for it, so I did, very gingerly and managed to reach my hole without falling and sliding on my arse into the audience. However, I felt like a right nana stuck in my little cavity doing stand-up, and was glad to escape the venue that night.

Our first daughter Maisie was born in 2001 at our local NHS hospital. Like our wedding, we strove to keep it quiet, although I did get a nice bunch of flowers from a tabloid newspaper congratulating me on the birth of my child — a week before it actually happened.

There then ensued the adjustment that needs to be made when a new baby comes into the house, and I'm sure I was no different from any other woman who has just given birth — almost comatose with tiredness, anxious and feeling like I lived in a parallel universe to everyone else. But we humans are an adaptable species and we cope because we have to.

I took six months off, then went back to a much reduced workload for a bit, which I still found hard. Being away from home for any length of time was a strain, so I tried to stay close enough to get back pretty quickly.

I realised fairly early on that as a woman with a baby in a buggy, one becomes all but invisible and I savoured being able to walk around, visit friends and wander through our local park with virtually no hassle at all. It was great. Tempted as I was to see if I could get away with it, I never had a crack at shoplifting.

Our second daughter Eliza was born in 2002, and despite our newly gained experience, it was a challenge coping with a baby and a toddler a year and a half apart. However, despite a lack of sleep, an increase in irritability and nights stretching to the length of a week, it was so lovely I didn't care.

Our daughters are now seven and nine, and happy at their local schools. It is slightly strange for them, I think, that I have a recognisable face, but they seem very pragmatic about it and handle the approaches I get from strangers with an admirable aplomb.

## The Girls

I have a simple philosophy when it comes to my children: I keep them out of the limelight. When I see reality shows on TV with celebrities' children in them, I feel rather sorry for the kids. It's not their choice to be there in front of a camera. I was very impressed, for example, when the oldest Osbourne daughter chose not to take part in the reality show about Sharon, Ozzy, Jack and Kelly. It's certainly worked for her. I don't even know her name and have no idea what she looks like.

I am constantly invited to events with the children, such as film premières, and it all looks so generous, exciting and fun. But, to use a hoary old cliché, there really is 'no such thing as a free lunch' and in payment for you having a lovely free day out, the press and the organisation entertaining you demand a piece of your life. And that means photos of the children and an encroachment into your family that I'm not prepared to countenance. When they're older and have more of an idea about things, they may berate me for this, but at the moment I feel I'm doing the right thing.

So that was a rather long-winded way of telling you that I am not going to furnish you with every personal detail of my daughters' development. I kept diaries during the first year of their lives and looking back through them, I realise what hard work it was, how tired I was, and also how anxious I was a lot of the time. I felt I was floundering about with not nearly as much knowledge as I needed. And because families are so far-flung these days, one cannot rely on the extended family in the way one used to be able to, and that goes for on-tap advice and support. Also, given that I was one of the dreaded 'older mothers', that inevitably meant that my own parents were not quite as sprightly as they would have been, had I been a bit younger. And because they live miles away they weren't on hand to take a turn round the park or do a bit of babysitting.

But I'm sure the first few years of our kids' lives were no different for us than for any other couples with young children. My diaries repeat over and over again that I was exhausted, up three or four times a night and ignorant of the right things to do:

E bought Maisie a Sex Pistols T-shirt that was pooed on within minutes.

Completely forgot about my bloody *Nursing Times* column.

Maisie blocked up, can't sleep, she's bloody exhausted. Me too.

Trying to think of ideas for novel, head feels like muzzy sponge in which ideas cannot germinate.

Trying to write, but head full of mashed potato because I am a mother.

Ordered pizza again.

Eliza up till 4. Me desperate to close my eyes, she desperate to play.

Bloody awful headache.

Midwife came round. So pleased to see her . . .
like a cross between the AA and a lifeboat.

Heard a story about a woman leaving her baby
in car seat on roof of car and driving off. (It was
OK, she stopped in time.) Feel I could have
managed that in my semi-comatose state.

Sounds a bit grim, doesn't it? But, of course, babies
are designed to be so delightful that you just cope and
it does get easier as they grow older. I remember asking
a friend what her well-earned holiday in Spain with
her toddler was like, only to be told, 'I spent two weeks
following her up and down some treacherous stone
steps.'

I can easily identify with that. Once babies become
mobile, you find yourself following them every minute
of the day, as accidents lie in wait round every corner.
Then that gets easier too, once they realise that sticking
their head down the toilet or playing in the knife
drawer will only bring tears.

I spent a lot of time in the park with the girls, which
is an odd mixture of stressful and a bit boring, if I'm

honest. They never want to leave! Even if you go with a friend, it's odds on their child will want to play right up the other end of the playground so you don't get much of a chance for adult conversation. Having said all that, I would have done an 'old woman who lived in a shoe' and had loads of kids if I wasn't so advanced in years.

As the kids approached school age the outside world began to encroach on them and it dawned slowly that I was slightly different from other mums. I can never forget Maisie coming home from school one day and asking me, 'Are you Jo Brand?' 'What makes you say that?' I asked. 'Everyone says you are,' she replied – and I had to admit I was.

# A Day in My Life

I don't really have typical days, but just recently at the beginning of this year I had so much to stuff into each day that I wondered if I was going to cope. Not only was I filming *Getting On*, the NHS comedy series, but I was also doing a programme called *Book Club* for Channel Four as well as trying to help the Labour Party shore up their potential vote, which was descending faster than a scary ride at Alton Towers.

One particular day – 8 February 2010, nearly finished me off . . .

**5.30 a.m.** I wander round in a semi-coma trying to remember what I need to take for filming *Getting On*.

Everyone is still asleep as I attempt to find some clothes that don't look as if I've just slept in them. I also need two sets of posh clothes for the *Book Club* on Channel Four, which I am filming after *Getting On* this evening. Look in posh clothes wardrobe and am forced to pick out some tops which I hate, as all of the others are either not clean or gathering dust in the dry cleaner's which I very rarely get to because I forget I've dropped stuff in there. Find something hideous and stuff it in a bag knowing that the charming wardrobe woman, Mia, at *Book Club* will run an iron over them for me.

As far as clothes for me to wear that day are concerned, so I don't have to turn up on the *Getting On* set with just my pants on, I plump for the least creased stuff on a mountainous pile. Leave the house at 6 a.m. in just about an alert enough state to drive. For this second series, *Getting On* is filmed in a deserted hospital in Plaistow in the East End of London, which involves going through the dreaded Blackwall Tunnel under the river.

The Blackwall Tunnel has the accolade of being jammed from five thirty in the morning till nine at night. I regret having to move our filming base from the previous hospital in Wandsworth, which was a lovely twenty-minute nip from home, whereas this journey takes an hour or even more at this time of the morning. I put the radio on and while in handy jam near my house, pour out very strong coffee from my sad old-lady flask to continue my alertness. Also have a back-up can of Red Bull if necessary.

I always drive myself everywhere as I like driving, I know all the routes round London better than a cabbie, I can have the radio on a station I like and, misanthrope that I am, I don't have to talk to anyone because I am miserable and half dead in the morning and this doesn't sit well with a cheery driver who's been up two hours more than me and is keen to chat. I flick about on the radio between Chris Evans' show on Radio 2 and Radio 4, when a report about either business/finance or Europe comes on and sends me back to Chris as I'm likely to drop off to sleep again.

**6 a.m.** I drive through a silent Peckham and Greenwich and head towards the Blackwall Tunnel. Oh, what a surprise – there's a traffic jam up ahead of me. We queue up to the lights for about 200 yards while I try to answer some texts from yesterday that I've forgotten about. A man behind beeps me because I haven't edged up twelve feet when the traffic has moved. Crawl onto the A2 and start heading towards the Tunnel. Not my favourite journey this, and I always find myself fantasising about water coming in or a fire when I'm down there, and look for secret doors I could escape out of. It's so long too. Seems to take ages to get through. Once on the other side, at least I am heading against the flow of the rush-hour traffic. It only takes me ten minutes to get to the hospital from here. I pull into a parking space, say hello to the security guy, and head in ten minutes early.

One of the marvels of filming is the breakfasts. As I come into the communal area I see, as usual, a veritable Roman-eat-till-you-explode feast of sausages, scrambled egg, beans, toast, mushrooms – the full English – and manage to grab a couple of sausages before I am hauled into make-up by Christine the make-up woman.

My make-up routine for Kim, the slobby, jaded nurse I play, is mercifully short, because we are trying to make the series as naturalistic as possible, so I just have a tiny bit of foundation and some eyebrows, and then I'm ready for action. Gathering more sausages en route, I make my way to the set, which is a perfect replica of a ward in a downmarket, slightly under-funded NHS hospital.

**8 a.m.** The first scene is a nice little one where I have to smoke in the toilet and speak to my husband 'Dave' on the phone. The toilet's reasonably big but not massive, and I am plonked rather uncomfortably on the edge of it so they can get me into shot. Also, it's absolutely bloody freezing, especially as I have a thin cotton nurse's dress and some alluring popsox on and have to pretend I'm in an overheated hospital. Everyone else seems to be wearing outdoor coats and jackets, the bastards.

Rather gloriously we have to do several retakes, which means several fags, a nice little break. Peter (Capaldi), the director and the cameramen Casper and Gary, a right cheeky pair, are located just outside the lav with Doug the delightful sound man, and we have a good laugh as I try and blow smoke out of the tiny open window. It's amazing how long these things take and I suppose half an hour later we finish and everyone moves onto the next scene.

I am not in the next two scenes so I get to wander about and have seventeen more sausages, read the papers and not do anything I'm supposed to be doing, like refreshing my memory for the two shows of the *Book Club* for Channel Four that I'm recording that evening. I take occasional trips to the lovely temporary toilets that are outside in the cold as none of the toilets inside are working and we have no water either.

I am then back on for three more scenes in a row which take place at the nurses' station, where I have to talk to Jo Scanlan, who is playing Sister Den, about dolphins, and then have an argument with Vicki Pepperdine, Dr Pippa Moore, about some money she owes my husband. We initially film one scene as written and then do the same scene again a little bit more freely. I can't help myself, I keep trying to put in one-liners, which I know I shouldn't because they look too contrived and will not get into the final edit, but it's a knee-jerk reaction, I'm afraid, and not being a proper actor but a comic, it's also my default position.

**1 p.m.** The midday meal comes upon us and I'm feeling knackered already as, however early I have to get up, I still can't go to sleep at a sensible time so I reckon I've had about five hours which is not enough for me. I need about twenty.

After eating, we piss about for a few minutes until we are called to have our make-up checked and go back to the 'ward'. In the afternoon we do more stuff at the nurses' station with me on the phone to someone who's looking for a bed and then me trying to get Sister Den to do my annual appraisal for me.

**5 p.m.** I have a special dispensation to shoot off early and get to Kennington in South London for two episodes of *Book Club*. I drive out of the hospital and try to take a short-cut and mess up and find myself in an area I don't recognise without a main road in sight. I then have to use my satnav, which tells me I am heading in exactly the opposite direction to where I'm supposed to be going. This has added a good ten minutes onto my journey and always happens to me when I'm supposed to get somewhere quickly.

Finally I am facing in the right direction and arrive in Kennington half an hour later than I'm supposed to. I stop at the shop and buy an evil-looking little bottle of something that's supposed to wake me up, but just makes me feel mildly irritable and anxious instead.

**6.15 p.m.** I arrive at Cactus TV in Kennington and am whisked into another make-up room where I am transformed from grubby nurse into international beauty . . . ish. I then get shooed up the corridor into the studio because I am so late, where my fellow conspirators await me. They are Dave Spikey (him off *Phoenix Nights* and a good egg to boot), Laila Rouass (off *Footballers' Wives*), very beautiful but such a down-to-earth laugh that you don't want to smack her in the gob with the envy of the aging stout old woman, Gok Wan, a one-man tornado of sound and light who, as an ex-fatty, feels like and is a real ally, and Nat Parker, the actor who plays the lead in the TV series *The Inspector Lynley Mysteries*, who is a likeable gentlemanly aristocrat with a twinkle in his eye.

Our special guest is Martine McCutcheon who I have bumped into over the years on such diverse shows as Jools Holland's *Hootenanny* and Comic Relief and she has her own book out to promote – *The Mistress*. We are reviewing a novel by Liz Jensen called *The Rapture* which I liked even though the plot went a bit bonkers at the end, so we discuss the book in a pretty relaxed way and try to find positives about it because we are not there to slag everything off.

By this point, the sofa on which I am sitting is temptingly comfy and it wouldn't take much for me to lie down and never get up again. I have a slight headache – that gritty-eye feeling you get when you're tired – and an inability to read the autocue with any degree of professionalism. It all seems to whiz by mercifully quickly and then we have a break between shows.

**8 p.m.** I go back to my dressing room for a wee and start to nod off on the toilet, not a good sign so I down my second little bottle of evil highly caffeinated energy drink and this seems to help. It also helps nipping outside for a fag with Gok, since if anyone can wake me up, it's him. He speaks at 900 miles an hour and I find myself being pulled out of my comatose state in an attempt to follow his very funny discourse about his family. This and my magic liquid seem to have pulled me back into the land of the living and I feel I can soldier on a bit more. I'm desperate to go home after the second show, but I have agreed to do a gig for some people from the Labour Party at 10.30 that night, giving me half an hour after the show to get my stuff together, drive over there and find the venue.

The next show sees Stephen Tompkinson as our guest and we are reviewing a sweeping novel set in Ethiopia and America in the 1930s called *Cutting for*

*Stone* by Abraham Verghese. It's very good so it's not difficult to find things to say about it. Stephen is good value for money, chatty and relaxed, and I have to be careful that I don't get so relaxed I start to keel backwards.

**10 p.m.** After the show has finished I rush to my dressing room and carefully fold my clothes – do I bollocks. I stuff them all into a carrier bag, because much as I would like to think of myself as one of those people who has designer clothes carriers, I simply am not and never will be. I was always the kid who turned up at school with my packed lunch in a Sainsbury's bag and suppose I always will be.

I get into the car feeling like a limp old piece of rag and seriously consider cancelling the Labour Party show. But I find I just cannot do it. My mum instilled the Protestant work ethic into me when I was a nipper and I am one of those people who still go to work if I am half dead. So I program the satnav for the Brompton Road and set off at rally-driving pace to try and find a night club called The Collection in SW3.

The first bit goes OK and I arrive at the Brompton Road in about twenty minutes and feel rather pleased with myself. Then, of course, I can't find the bloody venue. I drive up and down three times trying to spot the place. Finally, I start to panic and wonder if I'm ever going to get there. My satnav keeps saying, 'You have arrived at your destination,' and I keep replying, 'No, I haven't, you silly old cow. Do something.'

Eventually, I call someone at the Labour Party who says they'll get someone to call me, as I drive aimlessly up and down in the worst mood imaginable. Eventually someone does phone and says they have saved a parking space. They assure me that I am near by, and that someone else has been dispatched to find me. I pull into the kerb and in my wing mirror see some poor bloke in a suit legging it up the road at a hundred miles an hour. He is a Labour Party guy, not some besuited psychopath, so I let him in the car and we do a U-ey right in the middle of heavy traffic and I relish doing some rude signs as other drivers beep at me. We finally arrive outside the venue at number 264 and I have to park in a tiny space in front of a fifteen-strong welcoming committee. Inevitably I fuck it up and have to go in and out a few times. And then I am hardly out of the car when they descend on me, little knowing that I want to punch the first one who comes near me, I'm that stressed. I manage to smile through heavily gritted teeth and am escorted in.

**10.45 p.m.** It's even worse inside. There are hordes of people, all pissed, and the music is deafening (said grandma). As I'm late, I have about two seconds to prepare and then am shoved onto a makeshift stage to do my fifteen-minute bit. It goes by in a blur. I do some jokes about Cameron I have literally written on the back of a fag packet on my way, and then segue into my usual material which I know works.

Thank God, although it is noisy they are very friendly and seem to like me – which is fortunate because they were going to get it with both barrels if they didn't. I come off stage and am surrounded by alcohol fumes leaking out of very close faces. The owner asks me to come to a table with him for a drink, but I can do no more of anything sociable and plead exhaustion, although I can see he doesn't really believe me. However, I am past caring and head for the door, being waylaid every few feet or so to say hello to a very nice bunch of people. It's me that's the problem.

**11.45 p.m.** As I drive off I could cry I am so tired, and when I get home I drop everything on the floor, climb

*Left:* At the Royal Festival Hall, pretending to be intelligent

*Below:* At Selhurst Park, pretending Crystal Palace are winning

WWW.ANDYROBERTSPHOTOGRAPHY.CO.UK

*Right:* When I first started in comedy I didn't realise I was allowed to say no to looking like a twat

*Above: Through the Cakehole*, Fat People Sketch: coming to a chip shop near you. Before we tried to stuff ourselves into the Fiat . . .

*Above:* . . .We did all fit in once we'd had our torsos removed

*Below:* No cars behind me – must be coming last again

*Above:* Being made a Freeman of the City of London means I can now drive this man over London Bridge with a stick

*Right:*
Smiling
through the
political pain

*Above:* Trying to do acting
in *The Pirates of Penzance*

ALASTAIR MUIR

ANDY EARL

*Left:* Oh dear

*Right:* This may just be a dream I had

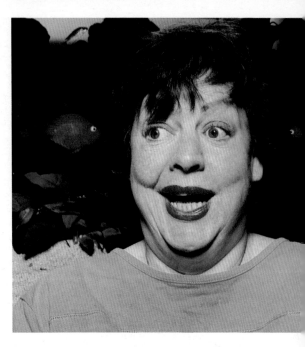

*Below:* On holiday with mates, still hung over at 8 o'clock in the evening

*above:* My family enjoying a British summer

*below:* My favouritest job. Judging the *Countryfile* photo competition

BBC COUNTRYFILE

Standing by some concrete looking gormless. For some reason they've put this photo in the National Portrait Gallery

into bed and pass out like I've been punched unconscious.

Just a small matter now of having to get up at 5.30
a.m. again . . .

# Mates

Friends are enormously important to me, especially long-standing ones, because they are the people who knew me before all this comedy stuff and therefore I value their opinion on things like whether I have turned into a showbiz arse or not.

Because of the immense cultural weight placed on being a so-called 'celebrity', people do react differently towards you, there is no getting round it. And so from the moment when I realised I was now someone whom people recognised off the telly, I found myself becoming warier and warier of those individuals who wanted to be my friend.

I know this is unfair of me and too cynical, because

on the whole, most people are friendly, honest and trustworthy – but when you look at those little messages in the tabloids that exhort you to phone in and grass up some celeb who's done something interesting, in some cases only pick their nose in the street, I feel it's important to be on your guard a bit. Add to that features like 'Spotted' in *Heat* magazine (a secret guilty pleasure of mine), which allows people to describe someone famous they saw and what they were doing, it does make you feel slightly under scrutiny. The irony of these items is that, most of the time, it's so dull. Are we really interested in the fact that Jimmy Carr was spotted talking into his mobile phone on Oxford Street? Not exactly an unusual thing to do, is it? Now if he'd been shoving it up someone's . . . well, you get the picture.

First of all, let's take those people who approach you at events. They often seem keen to let you know that: You're Not As Great As You Think You Are.

Well, it may come as a surprise, but I don't think I'm that great. I'm pleased and proud of the way my comedy career has turned out, but I like to think I'm not smug. However, there is a natural assumption on the part of some people that I must be flawed in the personality department. That may well be true, but I don't believe I am a diva in any way. This is because I did a 'normal' job for years and I know what it's like to earn a low wage for huge numbers of hours in a stressful job.

Secondly, I am perfectly well aware that some people may think I'm a demanding, petulant pain, so I actually go out of my way to prove them wrong. Even when I am feeling tired, fed up and ill, I still make an enormous effort to be polite and friendly. This doesn't wash with some people. They push and push, or they throw an insult out of the blue at you, which belies their initially friendly attitude. I did a book signing recently, and a woman who had queued for ages, finally got to the top of the line and informed me while I was signing her book that I was 'crap on *QI* the other night'. I just smiled and said, 'Oh, thanks,' which I think wrong-footed her a bit, but inside I was thinking, Oh, why don't you just fuck off, you stupid cow.

I myself wouldn't dream of being so rude to someone I don't know – and if you are thinking – Yes, you would, on stage – that is a completely different matter altogether. It's a performance and it has very little to do with me as a person, in the sense that all comedy performances are exaggerated versions of life. So when strangers say to me, 'I don't like you,' (which, believe you me, they do), or conversely, 'I'd love to be your friend,' they don't really mean me, they mean my stand-up act. This assumes that I go round all the time with the 'comedy' switch permanently turned on. Well, I don't. That would be too bloody exhausting for words and would royally piss off everyone I know.

I think a lot of people are rather disappointed when they meet me and when our ensuing interaction is not at the performance level of stand-up comedy.

One has a choice when one joins the world of show-business – to throw oneself headlong into it, or to observe from the sidelines – and the latter is what I chose to do. I have a slight horror of parties, full stop, let alone showbiz parties. I am regularly tongue-tied at these sorts of events as I cannot produce the sort of small talk that seems to be required unless I've had eight pints of lager, and then I tend to do and say quite a lot of things I regret the following day. It's just easier to steer clear of them.

I have made some very good friends from the comedy circuit over the years when we all started off, but on the whole I am not to be found at Elton John's annual shindig or premières and the like. I did once get invited to a party by Morrissey, whom I love, but I think he was seriously disappointed in the real me.

I feel much happier with a small group of longterm friends because I can relax, trust them, be myself with them and have a laugh.

My three best friends are Betty, Griffo and Edana, whom I have known since 1979 – hundreds of years. Betty, who lives round the corner from me, is the only one of us who managed to use her psychology degree to find a job in the field, and she now works as a senior psychologist. It's an absolute joy having a good friend so close at hand. We speak most days, and although we have enormously stressed lives, see each other all the time. I don't think I could survive if she wasn't around. I know I can tell her anything and she is absolutely trustworthy in every way, and we are as we always have been, completely in tune with each other.

Griffo lives in Swansea, which is a pisser, because I don't get to see her nearly as often as I'd like. She decided quite early on that she wanted to be an actress after we'd left college and has carved herself a fantastic career in an arena that is enormously competitive and cruel at times. We do our best to text/email/talk on the phone whenever possible. We work together too, as often as we can, and she recently played the part of the union rep in the comedy *Getting On*.

Edana is the third one of the triumvirate who worked

for many years in the Health Service, although she has always harboured a yen to write for TV. This opportunity came up recently for her and she is trying to convert her working life to fulltime writing but it's a very competitive field and it's taking a while.

We try to all get together once a year for a couple of days if we can, and our last trip was to a health spa . . . not my natural habitat, it has to be said. But it was pretty quiet and there was a lack of hassle from other punters. I did even, at one point, don my cozzie and get in the pool for some aquaerobics which I'd assumed would be a piece of piss. Blimey, it's actually quite hard work and I felt half dead afterwards. We also signed up for a 'brisk' walk (I realise the word 'brisk' should have been a clue) which was more like a bleeding route march in the Army. The main group pulled ahead of me many times, to my shame, and at one point I had to pretend I was off to find cover to have a piss while I cowered in a bush and had a sneaky fag.

And then, of course, there is my lovely friend Waggly who was diagnosed with MS while we were nurses together. She lives fairly close and is an inspiration to all of us as she has fought her illness tooth and nail, whilst devoting a lot of her time to her fellow sufferers. She's always available to help and has a gorgeous sunny optimistic outlook, given what a rough time she's had over the last few years.

## Showbiz Mates

Although it's difficult to meet and keep friends in this business because everyone is so bloody busy, and on my nights off I just want to flop over and spend time with the family, I do make an effort to spend time with the following mates from the comedy world.

## Kathy Burke

I think Kathy is a bloody genius and more than that, a fantastic person to spend time with. She is down to earth, funny and cynical, and a prime example of someone who has really struggled against the odds to become a leader in her field. We only meet a handful of times a year, but I always look forward to it enormously as I know I'm going to have a good time and spend a lot of it pissing myself laughing.

## Liza Tarbuck

Liza comes from comedy royalty and I first met her when we did a show up in Scotland together called *Win, Lose or Draw*. It was a joy to meet such a funny woman who could hold her own against all-comers. She is a right laugh too, has a very quick mind and doesn't take any shit from anyone.

## Dawn French

Dawn is absolutely lovely and totally comfortable in her skin. Sometimes I wonder how she has managed to remain so nice in the shark-infested waters of telly and show-business. She radiates a kind of positive light around herself and I defy anyone not to like her.

## Meera Syal

I first met Meera when she was in a sketch on the Channel Four show that I did, *Through the Cakehole*. I immediately liked her. She is bright, has a sardonic wit, and although we've managed to have quite a few elongated gaps in our friendship we are still clinging on and manage to see each other at least twice a year. It's difficult as we both have children and lives that are not conducive to meeting up, especially as we live at opposite ends of London.

## Jenny Eclair

Jenny Eclair is one of the biggest balls of energy I have ever met. She bursts into your personal space and will not be ignored. Her mind jumps all over the place and it's as if there is a pressure in her head to get more words out per minute than anyone else. She's very funny, very sarcastic and very lovable. We live quite close to each other, and almost every time I go to the local supermarket, I bump into her lurking somewhere in the aisles. Again, we struggle to maintain proper, regular contact but always have a really good gossip when we catch up.

## Ruby Wax

I am sure that the first time I met Ruby, she blanked me although she insists this isn't true, but we got over that and discovered we liked each other, although we are totally different. Ruby has a sharpness of mind that I simply don't possess and, like Jenny, she could talk the hind legs off any creature you care to mention. But there is a fondness between us and we like having big long laughing sessions together.

Hailing from Notting Hill, Ruby is not best keen on setting foot in Sarf London and treats it as if she were in the Bronx. She distracted me so much once when we were driving through South London that I hit the car in front. The driver got out, ready to remonstrate in a South London fashion i.e. quite cross, but on spotting both of us thought it was a hidden camera show and beat a hasty retreat.

Yes, I know you were expecting me to be holidaying with Elton and David or playing badminton with Posh and Becks, but I suspect I'm not quite glamorous enough. Bollocks – I don't suspect – I know.

# The Solitary World of Writing Books

The cliché that everybody has a novel in them is probably not true. I certainly don't think it was in my case.

However, once you achieve a certain level in the business of show, you do tend to get asked whether you'd like to write a book.

'Yes, one with lots of pictures and not much writing in it,' was always the response in my head.

Well, the offer did come my way in the early nineties, and based on a book that had been published a year or so before, about the hundred greatest men in history, I decided I would have a bash at my own list.

The first book was called *A Load of Old Balls*, and although I had some characters in there that you might expect, like Jesus, I also added a few like Ronald McDonald. I enjoyed writing it, the structure was simple and it was like fifty short pieces of stand-up.

This then led to the second book – *A Load of Old Ball Crunchers* – a list of fifty great women in history.

I am not in the slightest bit organised, so my approach to writing these two books was pretty chaotic and depended on things like how hungover I was, what was on telly and whether I felt like it. Some days if I was in the mood I could write for twelve hours; other days, after an hour and a half I'd have gone stir crazy and had to go out.

It was the three novels that I found most difficult. Having had a break from writing for a few years and got married and had children, when I was approached by Headline to write a novel I thought it would be a good idea to accept, because my eldest daughter was still pretty much a baby and it meant I could stay in wearing my nightie and sit at the laptop composing great prose while rocking the cradle with one of my feet.

Of course it's never how you expect it to be and after a couple of months I found myself rather resenting the huge amount of work it entailed. A novel is such a massive undertaking. It's like doing thirty really long essays, all run together. And you wonder where you are going to find enough words to put in it.

I decided to write about areas that I knew.

So my first book, *Sorting Out Billy*, was set in South-East London where I was from and involved three friends, one of whom was a budding stand-up comic (unsurprisingly). One of the three friends had a boyfriend who was violent towards her and it fell to the other two to try and sort him out. It is a comedy book and you may question why I thought domestic violence was a suitable topic for comedy. In itself of course it's not funny, but every base aspect of human nature has a darkly comic side to it and this was what I was trying to achieve.

The next novel was called *It's Different for Girls* and was set in Hastings, again an area that I am very familiar with because I spent my teenage years there. Rather conveniently, I set it in the seventies when I was a teenager – hence demolishing with one swipe of my pen as it were, the need for ploughing through archives of teenage lives in that decade.

And finally, my third book – which is my favourite – was called *The More You Ignore Me*. It was set in

Herefordshire, where I spend a lot of time, and involved the two ends of the fan spectrum within one rural family. To write it, I drew on my knowledge and experience of mental illness. It seems that now I may have exhausted my personal repertoire, so if I ever write another novel I may well have to spend the first few months doing research.

The first novel took six months, the second six weeks and the third two years – and all of them had their attendant problems. It's unlikely that I will ever give up my career as a comic to become a fulltime writer. It's too lonely and there's too much opportunity to skive off.

I have also contributed to other books, including many charity ones. A very popular way of raising money is to produce a celebrity cookbook, and in many ways I am the worst person to come to, because I hate cooking and I like eating very boring food. So I have to rack my brains every time, as I'm sure no one would be too impressed by a recipe for cheese on toast or spag bol, both of which I'm very good at. Well, they're the *only* things I'm good at, to be truthful.

My favourite contribution of all time was to the *QI Annual 2008*. I was asked to do a page called 'Fags of the World' and was sent a sheet of paper with about a hundred packets of cigarettes on it and told to provide a by-line for each one.

This was tremendous fun to do and enabled me to write captions, say for a packet of Russian cigarettes, with the words: *'Perfect after you've shagged your best friend's husband.'*

# A Nasty Habit

Ending the last chapter with a cigarette – a Russian one, to boot – leads me neatly into this chapter on the pleasures and perils of tobacco.

We are all absolutely certain by now that SMOKING IS A BAD THING. And that's not just for you as an individual, but also for the people around you into whose faces and lungs you may be blowing your smoke. There was a golden era in the forties and fifties when people were blissfully ignorant of the dangers of smoking and assumed it to be the most sophisticated and attractive habit in the world. Then gradually, through research, it began to dawn on us that perhaps it wasn't the health-giving habit everyone assumed it to be. Smokers metamorphosed from urbane creatures into scuzzy lepers, who were not only damaging themselves but their loved ones too.

Of course, as a fourteen-year-old schoolgirl I didn't know anything about this when I started smoking. It was a simple act of teenage rebellion, combined with the boredom of a very long bus journey to school on which several of us would produce our tiny little packets of ten Number Six out of our satchels and try to look like we knew what we were doing as we attempted to direct the stream of smoke out through the tiny slot of window on the bus that we could actually get open.

After Number Six I moved onto Rothmans, whose ad showed the arm of a pilot at the controls of a plane, thereby implying that you could be something as dashing as a pilot if you sucked on these babies too.

According to Mr Sigmund Freud, smoking is an oral pursuit and I won't bore you with the theories, but it seems to me that smoking is used by a lot of people to calm their nerves, firstly by giving them something to do with their hands and secondly by supplying them with some nicotine to soothe their anxiety.

I have worked in two professions that worship smoking: nursing and comedy. It's amazing how many nurses and doctors smoke, given that they, more than anyone, should be well-versed in the potential dangers. But many dedicated smokers play the lottery game of assuming it will not be them who suffer the longterm effects, and cling rather pathetically to stories of stalwart elderly people in their nineties who have smoked eighty a day throughout their lives and can still run a marathon.

As a nurse I can't believe now, when I look back to my days in the Emergency Clinic, that we were actually allowed to smoke in the nurses' office, where you could sit down and have a break or a cry after someone had hit or abused you. The place was thick with the fug of smoke and must have been really unpleasant for the non-smokers, but your smokers tend to be a selfish lot so we just carried on puffing away.

Similarly in comedy, in the good old bad old days, dressing rooms would be stuffed full of nervous comics waiting to go on, dragging on their fags as if they were full of oxygen. Audiences smoked too, so everywhere had a blue-tinged mist hanging over it – and that kind of felt right and matched the atmosphere of tension and expectation.

As the smoking ban started to bite, I found myself having an increasingly adolescent attitude towards the rules and trying to get away with smoking in as many non-smoking areas as I could. When I toured Australia, we deliberately booked on an airline that still let you smoke, as the thought of a fourteen-hour and then a seven-hour flight did my head in anyway, let alone being forbidden to have a fag.

For me, smoking is a way of tackling social anxiety. These days, I don't drink so much or so regularly, as I don't think I could function as a parent if I got pissed too often – sorry to deliver such a bombshell. Therefore my life has followed a pattern of drinking absolutely bloody loads in short bursts and behaving quite badly on a number of occasions, but always having a fairly consistent intake on the fag front. When my anxiety rises, so does my smoking, and at social events like parties – or gigs, of course – I do actually find it helps me feel slightly less wobbly.

During my twenties and thirties, it didn't really occur to me to give up, but when I decided I wanted to have children I got the most almighty lecture from my GP and decided to stop. I did this by making a cutting-down plan over three weeks, cutting down from forty a day to three on the final day. The last days were almost worse than having given up, because the gap between cigarettes seemed to stretch like an eternity of doom ahead of me and I found myself counting down the hours, minutes and seconds to when I could have another one. I didn't use any chemical aids like that chewing gum.

On the final day I had a last cigarette, attempting desperately to smoke the filter, and then stopped. It was bloody awful. I tried to cut out things that I associated with smoking, like talking on the phone to friends for hours on end, going to pubs, and Mark Lamarr, who had been a good old smoking buddy for years.

However, I couldn't actually cut out Mark Lamarr as I had a gig in Birmingham at the Glee Club two days into the new fag-free regime. I had decided to aid my giving up with some special medication known as Murray Mints ('too good to hurry mints') and seemed to be getting through about three bags a day. When I arrived at the Glee and walked into the dressing room it smelled like a war zone to me. I had been free of smoke for two days and it was a bit of a shock. Also, I was worried that without the crutch of a cigarette, my act would fall to pieces. However, I didn't give in and did my first ever smoke-free gig.

Up until this point, I also used to smoke on stage – which seems like some weird surreal dream now. If I'm honest, my set was a bit shit, but better than I'd expected. I'd thought I might just break down on stage and sink to my knees crying, but I got through it – and as soon as I walked off stage made a run for the door, back to my smoke-free world. There is no doubt I was irritable over a number of weeks and possibly months, but eventually I realised I could live with it and settled into a fag-free existence.

That fag-free existence lasted for five years, although occasionally I would catch a whiff of someone's cigarette and be carried back nostalgically to those days when my powers of self-denial were rubbish. I suppose I just tried to be pleased that my powers of self-denial had been strengthened.

My willpower did crack, though, five years on. This was down to a stressful period in my life consisting of too much work, some family problems and being pissed. I was at a launch party for Paul O'Grady's latest book and for once I'd left the car at home. Normally, I use the car to stop myself binge drinking, as having got away with drinking and driving once I knew I would never do it again. I don't normally go to things like this, but I'm very fond of Paul and I needed a night out.

Having imbibed enough alcohol to lower the resistance of the Pope, I looked at a friend's cigarette and found myself saying, 'Can I have a puff?' My mate Alan

Davies gave me the beady eye (he has always tried to stop my smoking excesses) but, fuelled by enough vodka and tonics to render an entire office Christmas party unconscious, I turned away and took a drag on my friend Andy's cigarette. Blimey, was it lovely. And that was the beginning of the end. At the next party I had a whole one and over the next six months, passed the point of no return by eventually buying my own packet – a sure sign I was on the road to rack and ruin.

So, sadly, I am a smoker again, but this time round I seem to have a little more control than I did and am planning to try and tackle it again. Don't know where, don't know when, but I'm sure I'll meet the non-smoking me again some sunny day.

# Scoffing in the Light: My Favourite Books

What I like best in life is reading books, preferably accompanied by a little light scoffing. It is something that has not been easy to do since I've had kids, as finding time to read when there are eight thousand other things to do is like putting time aside for darning. That is the main reason why I agree to judge book awards, as I know it will force me to read and that I will love it. And I do. Books have been really important to me throughout my life, and the books I love best which have really stayed with me are the following:

## *The Ragged Trousered Philanthropists*
## by Robert Tressell

This is one of the first books written at the turn of the last century which is actually about the working classes. It is quite a dense, difficult read and I rejected it as a teenager, because there just seemed too many long words on the page. It is about a group of builders doing up a house for a rich bloke in 'Mugsborough', a fictional town which is actually based on Hastings, where I spent a lot of time as a teenager.

The group of builders all have very different personalities and political views, and to some extent are caricatures, but the story gives a real insight into the lives of the poor, as men are laid off, families struggle with feeding their children and preventable tragedies occur. The idea of socialism rears its head through one of the characters who is a committed leftie. *The Ragged Trousered Philanthropists* also has a very poignant connection for me in that my lovely brother-in-law Paul, who died at a relatively young age just after our daughter Maisie was born, and who taught English Literature at Oxford Brookes University, was an expert on this book. It is one of the must-reads for anyone who has vaguely left-wing views, and must have been a breath of fresh air for readers, who at that time had only been treated to the lives of the middle and upper classes with whom they would have found it very hard to identify.

I don't dismiss all that wonderful literature out of hand, however, as I think novels like *Pride and Prejudice* are glorious and so is anything by Charles Dickens, although the many working-class characters in his novels tend not to be shot through with a political ethos.

I'd urge you to have a crack at *The Ragged Trousered Philanthropists*. It's very sad and depressing in parts, but it gives you an invaluable glimpse into the lives of working people, before we had unions to protect them. And although unions these days, having been somewhat decimated by Margaret Thatcher, are frowned upon because of their excesses, to me they retain an essential role for the worker who needs to be shielded from the completely profit-orientated approach of big business.

Blimey, you're probably thinking, you sound like a Commie. I am not a Communist but I feel very strongly that any civilised society should have in place organisations that look after the lives of so-called 'small' people who don't have any power or protection.

### *A Christmas Carol* by Charles Dickens

And so to Dickens. I find it very hard to pick out a favourite as I particularly love *Great Expectations*, *David Copperfield* and *Barnaby Rudge*, but *A Christmas Carol* is such an optimistic book, and its images filled my childhood. I'm sure I don't need to tell you that the main character is Scrooge, a grumpy, mean-spirited misanthrope who treats his employees and everyone else he comes into contact with like dirt. The story is about his metamorphosis from miser to cheery philanthropist and general good geezer through his contact with a series of ghosts who show him his past, present and future. From talking about the struggling working classes as a group he thinks 'should die and decrease the surplus population', he turns into a beneficent old man keen to help those who are finding life intolerable.

If only it were so easy to get the bad-tempered old self-servers in our society to read this and change their lives in the way Scrooge did, but I still hold out some hope. Programmes like *Secret Millionaire* (although obviously there is a slightly cynical televisual edge to them), in which some loaded person is sent off to a grim part of Britain to find out about the lives of poor working, and unemployed, people also adds to the stock of encouraging a kinder attitude to what many people would have us think are feckless cheating ruffians.

**The Faber Book of Reportage**, edited by John Carey
This bloody marvellous book is a series of eye-witness reports of events in history told from various viewpoints. So there are such diverse pieces as Charles Dickens witnessing a hanging, reports from soldiers in the First and Second World Wars, and some heart-breaking accounts of children working in factories in the Victorian era.

The earliest reports go all the way back to Pompeii and the devastation caused by the eruption of Vesuvius, and come up as far as the unseating of the shoe-loving Imelda Marcos and her husband as they are chucked out of power in the coup in the Philippines.

My favourite piece is the report of a group of rowdy women in medieval England who would go to jousts dressed up as men and generally cause trouble by getting pissed and being lary. Nice to see some medieval ladettes giving it large.

The pleasure gained from reading this book was increased tenfold when I was on a Radio 4 programme about favourite books in which three of us swapped books and then commented on each other's choice. One of the other guests was Jonathan Meades, an author and what they call 'a cultural commentator', and he had a right good old sneer at my choice of the book of reportage, rubbishing its historical validity, because each piece was a subjective view. As I tend to think of 'cultural commentators' as rather smug types like critics (who are they to tell the rest of us what we should and shouldn't think, anyway?) it made me feel even more fond of this book.

### *Moments of Reprieve* by **Primo Levi**

This again is an optimistic book which covers one of the most shameful periods in our global history, the genocide of the Jews by Hitler during the Second World War. You may find it difficult to imagine that anything positive could come out of this truly harrowing and agonising time. The book is set in Auschwitz and consists of a series of essays by Primo Levi, who himself had been a prisoner in that concentration camp. It details significant moments when a ray of hope shone into his life of struggle and degradation due to small acts of kindness from the other people there, whether it was another prisoner saving tiny bits of food for him, or a normally brutalised guard committing an uncharacteristic act of compassion. I found this book a fascinating read in its attempt to glean some small comfort from the all but destroyed altruism of certain individuals.

Primo Levi suffered terrible 'survivor's' guilt in later life, and ended up killing himself, many years after the war. However, this book and the others that he wrote on the same subject are a small pool of light in the gloomy theatre of human brutality.

## *In the Springtime of the Year* by Susan Hill

Are you depressed enough now? Well, don't be too hopeful that things are going to take an upward turn just yet, because this book, by one of my favourite authors, Susan Hill, is not exactly full of laughs. It's set in the English countryside in a place very similar to where I grew up, and details the life of a woman whose husband is killed in a tree-felling accident right at the beginning of the novel.

The rest of this beautifully written story takes us through her grief and then eventual acceptance of her widowhood. It's the sort of book you can immerse yourself in, particularly if you love the countryside as

I do, since every page brings some new and exquisite description of the changing face of rural life throughout the seasons.

As my mum said to me once, 'Don't read *The White Hotel* by D.M. Thomas if you're feeling depressed.' I did, and true to her prediction I felt a whole lot worse, so this is not a book to read if your life is a bit grim. Save it till you feel better and then you can wallow in its misery.

## *One Flew Over the Cuckoo's Nest* by Ken Kesey

I'm sure this book contributed towards me wanting to become a psychiatric nurse – not so I could become like Nurse Ratched the psychopathic nightmare who runs the ward, you understand! No, I suppose I wanted to be an antidote to her.

*One Flew Over the Cuckoo's Nest* details the admission of one Randle McMurphy to a psychiatric unit in America – a complex man, I would say, with a personality disorder – who proceeds to lay waste to the rigidly organised totalitarian regime of the ward created by Nurse Ratched. His cheeky, unorthodox troublemaking throws the ward into confusion as narrated by a Native American patient who, wordless and inscrutable, floats on the periphery of the action and observes the descent of McMurphy into a kind of hell.

This is a gripping description of the isolated universe of the psychiatric hospital in those days when the staff could pretty much do what they liked to control unacceptable behaviour. It's also really funny and touching, and is to me the definitive handbook of how *not* to be a psychiatric nurse. Of course, the iconic film starring Jack Nicholson, which sees the action from a different perspective, is easily as good as the book – a rare phenomenon in cinema and literature – and Jack Nicholson will be forever linked with the cheeky McMurphy for me.

## *1984* by George Orwell

George Orwell has written so many great books that I find it difficult to choose a favourite. I love *Animal Farm*, a demolition of the totalitarian state if ever there was one, and *Down and Out in Paris and London*, with which I have a vague connection in that the 'spike' or doss house in which the narrator stays was in fact in Camberwell, and was a place to which we would refer rough sleepers from the Emergency Clinic.

I chose *1984* though, because it's a literary classic

and contains pertinent warnings for us all as we move towards the future. There are so many words and phrases in it too, which have become part of our everyday language, such as 'Thought Police' and 'Big Brother'. The novel tells the story of the hapless civil servant Winston Smith as he attempts to fight the power of the all-seeing Big Brother and gain some individuality and freedom. One very telling piece in it describes the newspapers that are read by the 'proles' – the amorphous group of so-called 'lowlifes' who scrabble around on the fringes of society, poor and under-educated. These papers are more like comics and take the minds of the proles off anything more important that may be going on. Weirdly, apparently, when the *Daily Mail* serialised *1984*, they left out this bit.

I championed *1984* in one of those BBC *The Nation's Favourite*-type shows, and I think *1984* came third or fourth. I made a programme about it and we did much of the filming in a disused tube station near Green Park in Central London. God, it was terrifying being that far underground in the dark with cobwebs and dust. I was pleased to get back up and breathe the air, even London's dirty, polluted sort.

The infamous Room 101 came out of Orwell's time

at the BBC, and we managed to visit it halfway through its demolition and redecoration. No rats there though, thankfully.

### *The Children of Dynmouth* by William Trevor

William Trevor is a lovely Irish writer whose writing I find easy to read and quirky. *The Children of Dynmouth* is an arresting novel about a very strange, rather disturbed teenage boy who lives in a typical, sleepy Dorset seaside town whose occupants are seemingly content and unsullied by scandal. Our anti-hero Timothy Gedge decides he wants to win a prize in the tableau competition at the church fete, so having decided he is going to portray the Brides in the Bath murders, he sets about gathering the various bits and pieces he will need to achieve this aim. As he has no money, he needs to beg, steal or borrow a bath and a wedding dress among other things. He does this through a series of encounters with the town's occupants, in which he uses information about them to persuade them to cough up the goods, and in so doing pruriently uncovers the seedier side of the so-called respectable town-dwellers' lives.

I have always thought that beneath the veneer of respectability of some of our more picturesque areas lurk many unsavoury stories waiting to be told, and in this novel, elderly spinsters and old colonels alike are shown to be hiding secrets they would rather not reveal. Don't read this if you are posh and well-respected and hiding an unpleasant secret, as this will only depress you.

# Scoffing in the Dark: My Favourite Films

It has to be said, spare-time-wise, I have pretty un-demanding hobbies. Books, films and theatre are my big pleasures, and over the years I have spent many happy hours sat in cinemas in the dark crying, laughing and stuffing very unhealthy food down my gullet... bliss. Here are my favourite films.

### Local Hero

This Bill Forsyth film is an absolute joy, with a cracking soundtrack by Mark Knopfler. It tells the story of an oil company executive visiting a beautiful coastal village in Scotland to try and persuade the villagers to allow their unspoiled region to be used for a new oil plant. They are offered huge sums of money and are all keen, apart from one old geezer who has lived on the beach itself for years.

This is a perfect film for me as I remain anti-American to my core: their aggressive brand of expansionism and the ruining of the beauty of many natural areas has often pissed me off over the years. Eventually in the film, the boss Burt Lancaster comes over to try and persuade the old man to cave in and we are treated to an array of wonderful comedy characters played by actors including Denis Lawson and Peter Capaldi.

Many years after I first saw the film I met Peter Capaldi at a 'do' at the London Studios and got the opportunity to tell him how great I thought he was. I never find it easy to do this as it always sounds so wanky. However, we eventually got to work together on *Getting On* as he directed it, and it was a real pleasure to spend time with the comedy genius who plays one of my favourite characters, Malcolm Tucker.

### True Stories

*True Stories* is a film made by David Byrne of Talking Heads, and it features him as a cowboy-hatted stranger visiting a small town called Virgil in Texas which is preparing for some celebrations for the 150th anniversary of its founding. It was one of the very early roles for the magnificent John Goodman from *Roseanne*, who plays a lonely bachelor looking for love, and the film builds to his performance of a song at the celebration. The film is an idiosyncratic visual and musical feast, which completely confirms David Byrne's genius. Every song is memorable and it's a very funny and touching film.

### *Cabaret*

This is Liza Minnelli's finest moment, playing Sally Bowles, an American performer in Berlin in the thirties, in the film based on the novel *Goodbye to Berlin* by Christopher Isherwood. The songs are so evocative, and as a relationship develops between her and a slightly staid English teacher played by Michael York, we follow the progress of the rise of the Nazi Party, whose increasing threat and inexorable march towards power is not only reflected in the action of the film, but also within the songs that Sally Bowles sings at the Kit Kat Club, a down-at-heel cabaret filled with an array of unsavoury characters.

The performance of Joel Grey as the maître d' is

unforgettable, and I rewatch the film every few years to soak up its genius. I remember once being in a car going to a show out of town with Hattie Hayridge, and we were playing the soundtrack in the car. When it got to the song 'Tomorrow Belongs To Me' which is sung in a chilling scene outside a country tavern and encourages, one by one, a series of Aryan young men to stand up and pledge themselves to Nazism, I'm afraid Hattie and I started doing Nazi salutes . . . much to the puzzlement and dismay of the occupants of the car next to us at the traffic-lights.

A couple of years ago, I went to see Julian Clary play the maître d' in the West End. It was a great performance and I also got to see Julian's bum, which is not something huge numbers of women can say, I'm sure.

### Great Expectations

David Lean's iconic version of the Dickens novel was a big feature of my childhood, mainly because the chilling opening scene in which Pip meets the criminal Magwitch in a graveyard scared the shit out of me and stopped me sleeping for many nights. John Mills is absolutely delightful as the grown-up Pip, and the images of the film have stayed with me for many, many years and fostered a love of Dickens' novels that I certainly didn't have when I first saw it as a seven year old.

## To Kill a Mockingbird

Gregory Peck as Atticus Finch, a lawyer representing a black man accused of rape in 1930s Alabama, is my all-time favourite character. Considering most of the output of studios of the time was unchallenging, morally bland stuff about lurve or adventure, this film is a groundbreaker in so many ways and it opened the debate about racism for many Americans whose shameful history needed to be explored.

All the performances are amazing, from that of the little girl called Scout to the accused Tom Robinson, and if you're not a reader prepared to tackle the book, at least see the film.

## Terms of Endearment

*Terms of Endearment* is in some ways one of the most slushy films of the last fifty years, but it is also hugely funny as well, featuring an Oscar-winning performance from Shirley MacLaine as the tight-arsed, snobbish mother of the central character played by Debra Winger, who is dying of leukaemia; and Jack Nicholson as a pissed, sardonic ex-astronaut. In parts it is heartbreaking and in others hysterical as Shirley MacLaine's dignity is endlessly compromised by Jack. Makes you want to hunt down and marry a pissed ex-astronaut.

### Riff Raff

*Riff Raff*, directed by Ken Loach, is a film by that most unusual of creatures, a film-maker with a political conscience. It's set in London in the Thatcherite era and tells the story of a group of builders converting a wrecked NHS hospital into luxury flats. It stars Robert Carlyle, Ricky Tomlinson and Emer McCourt and has a strong political message underlying the many unparalleled comical scenes. The foreman is the best swearer in the business and equals Malcolm Tucker in *The Thick of It* for his obscene rants about laziness. I have a tenuous connection with Emer McCourt who played Robert Carlyle's girlfriend Susan, because she ended up directing *Human Traffic*, a film in which I had a don't-blink-or-you'll-miss-me part. In fact, you did miss me, because I was edited out of the final cut. No idea why, assume I was shit, don't ever ask about those things.

### Twin Town

I am a huge adolescent, because there's nothing I like better than relentless, creative swearing, and you get massive amounts of it in this very funny Welsh film. Starring Rhys Ifans, it tells the story of twin brothers attempting to get justice for their father who has been injured in a work accident. There are drugs, local gangsters and Welsh male voice choirs, a cameo by Keith Allen whose brother Kevin directed it, and an hysterically funny scene with my very good mate Griffo playing a prostitute. It's bloody brilliant, and if you want to upset your slightly uptight grandma, send her a DVD for Christmas.

# Trying Not to Scoff in the Dark: My Favourite Plays

One of the great joys of living in London is the number of theatres that are on our doorstep. To be honest, I don't get out much, but I do try and make it to the theatre as often as I can. First of all, it's such a unique experience: no one show is the same as another, and the actors are right there in front of you, sweating their bits off to bring you a transcendental experience that I find stays with you much longer than a film does. Also, there's nothing quite as bad as bad theatre – it's really, really, *really* bad. But when it's good it's unbeatable.

Going to the theatre should not be a posh/middle-class thing either, but should be there for everyone. I know that prices are prohibitive, but when I was a nurse I used to go because I would rather have seen one play than five films.

Plays that have left me spellbound are:

### Candide

Now who would have thought that an eighteenth-century satire by Voltaire could have been turned into a successful musical? Well, not me for a start-off, but I was persuaded to see it because it had such stunning reviews, and it is an understatement to say that I was not disappointed. Beautifully and imaginatively staged, it starred that giant of the theatre Simon Russell Beale, whom you may never have heard of because he so rarely gets his gob on the telly.

I won't bother to go into the plot of *Candide*, because you might decide to drop off, but suffice it to say that the songs were sing-along-y brilliant, it was funny, moving, interesting, enlightening and sharp as a knife – and as soon as it finished I wanted to see it all through again and again.

I met Simon Russell Beale in the corridor of the National Theatre once and I nearly fainted, because of being in touching distance of such genius. And then he said to me he was a fan of mine, and I'm not being a falsely modest nana here but I was struck dumb, so Simon, I'm an even bigger fan of yours.

### As You Like It

Shakespeare's a difficult one because you do him at school and most English teachers only manage to instil in you a hopeless antipathy towards his plays, causing you to shy away from them in the future, because most of the time you have absolutely no idea what the bloody hell the characters are going on about.

However, once in a while you see something which underlines Shakespeare's genius, and this was the case with *As You Like It* at the National Theatre, once again starring the incomparable Simon Russell Beale. It was funny (which is no mean feat with a Shakespearean comedy), I understood it, and lapses into my own mind, in which I compiled a shopping list, or tried to remember all the Doctor Whos in order, were rare.

The same happened some years ago when I went to see Dustin Hoffman in *The Merchant of Venice*. God bless him, Dustin's accent wandered round America and Europe for quite a while until it settled in Italy, but

Geraldine James, who played Portia, was amazing. I particularly noticed that she did the 'quality of mercy' speech with a feeling and emphasis I had never heard before, and which put the whole thing into the most easily understandable context. Because it is a speech that drama students regularly trot out with all the emotion of a tranquillised slug, to hear it done proper by a proper grown-up actress was an absolute joy.

## Art

This play by Yasmin Reza is a wonder. It's very funny and it gave comics such as Jack Dee and Frank Skinner an opportunity to get a foot in the door of West End theatre. The play concerns three friends, one of whom buys a very expensive painting which is basically just a white canvas, and the feelings thrown up by the attitudes of the three main characters is the basis of the drama. Doesn't sound like much, does it? It's a masterpiece though, and if you get a chance . . .

Now, you may think, having heard me describe my three favourite hobbies (accompanied by the fourth i.e. scoffing), that I indulge only in high-falutin' middle-class pursuits. In which case I should tell you that I love *Big Brother* and all reality shows, I read celeb mags to wash my brain and give me respite from having to think too much, and I am addicted to a stupid game on my mobile called *Bubble Boom Challenge* which I surreptitiously play in boring meetings in the vain hope that people will think I'm sending a very, very import-ant text. Since I learned to play the organ I try and keep that up, but I am like a ten year old: I never practise apart from the day before I have a lesson and I deliberately choose things to play that are very easy, so I am not challenged in any way.

# Politricks

I have always been interested in politics and I owe this to my parents who, I am sure I have already mentioned, met at a Young Socialists' event and constantly talked politics at home. In fact, in 1993 my mum stood as the Labour candidate in the Ludlow local elections. Given that Ludlow is one of the strongest bastions of Tory supremacy, she was never going to get anywhere, but we were all really proud of her. I have never voted anything except Labour, and so I suppose it was inevitable that I would get stuck into politics as a comic.

I missed out on the Red Wedge stuff, because it coincided with the very early part of my comedy career and I was not considered high-profile enough, I suppose, to be asked to do stuff. If you don't know what Red Wedge was, it was a sort of loose music and comedy collective involving such characters as Billy Bragg, Ben Elton, Madness, Phill Jupitus and the like. It was set up to try and prevent Margaret Thatcher winning another election in 1985, but sadly didn't manage it, and its members eventually drifted apart some five years later.

I never got involved in local politics, although I was a member of the Labour Party, because I found political meetings on that level rather difficult to cope with due to the structure and bureaucracy. It seemed to me that phrases like 'Subsection B part 14' were designed to make you go bonkers and so I supported from the sidelines rather than getting stuck in.

However, as my career moved on a bit I began to receive calls asking me to support the Labour Party in various ways.

The first event I remember being involved in was a party at Brown's in Central London (not Gordon, a restaurant), which was a fundraiser for the Labour Party. Michael Foot, my hero, was there as were Gordon Brown and Neil Kinnock. I had written a comedy version of *The Red Flag*. This was the Labour Party's anthem for many decades, but apparently played down during the Blair years.

My comedy version started with the line: 'Neil Kinnock's hair is deepest red, though most of it's not on his head,' and finished with a line about Gordon Brown's hair looking a bit shit. (Yes, not the cutting edge of political satire, I'll admit.) I was aware while singing it that Gordon Brown had come into the room just as I got to the line about his hair. It flashed through my mind to drop it, as I didn't want to offend him, but it's hard to find a whole new line to end a song instantly so I carried on and he didn't seem to mind. And also, the poor sod's had far worse abuse since then.

I did many benefits for the Labour Party over the years and supported them in any way I could. I wasn't too happy when New Labour got in, but one has to be realistic about these things. Old Labour was completely unelectable and had not been in power for years, and politics was turning into a game that was all about image rather than principles and policies. Sizeable numbers of the electorate, as we know, are not really interested in the cut and thrust of politics and base their judgements on selfish local issues, so I suppose Blair in some ways was a necessary evil.

Margaret Thatcher was someone I find it difficult

to say anything positive about. Her time as Prime Minister was particularly depressing because it was such a huge thing that she was our first woman Prime Minister and as a woman I really wanted to be proud.

But I found her totally impossible to understand as a person. She seemed humourless, inflexible in her thinking, schoolmistressy, cold and old-fashioned. I think some of the really telling things she said over the years marked her out as someone who was a representative of a culture that encouraged people to be just out for themselves – and this goes some way to explaining why a new type of alternative comedy developed. Here are some key phrases of hers:

**'There is no such thing as society'**
Well, what a bloody ridiculous thing to say. You cannot avoid the fact that there are interconnections between groups of people that constitute some sort of loose grouping we call society. I think this was more wishful thinking than anything else on Margaret Thatcher's part. This was an attempt to reframe the political landscape and to encourage people to stand on their own two feet without the safety net that I consider a truly democratic society should provide for its citizens. Therefore, she was interested in the state being pared

back to the minimum, and those who struggled with poverty, unemployment, disability, mental health problems, single motherhood or just an inability to fit in, could either sort themselves out or pull themselves together or whatever the pointless instruction was.

In order to do this paring back, I think that Margaret Thatcher had to shift her perspective on people with problems and view them as somehow feckless, responsible for their situation or in some way criminal. I am not denying that there are always going to be those who misuse the funds the state provides for people in trouble, but does that mean that all those who are deserving of some help in difficult times should be denied that help because some scumbags abuse the system?

Coupled with that, there are plenty of very wealthy people who prove themselves equally dishonest and grasping, and who eschew their responsibilities as far as tax is concerned by hiding their money in foreign bank accounts or creating dodgy companies to hide their true wealth. We also know, following the uncovering of the recent expenses scandal amongst MPs, that there is a percentage of people in every walk of life who will take advantage of what is on offer and illegally claim money that they do not deserve.

I must admit, when the whole expenses scandal came to light, it really depressed me, particularly in the case of Labour MPs. I cling on to a belief that Labour MPs are the true representatives of the working classes, and to find out that they also had their snouts in the trough was extremely galling. That's not to say that the Conservatives and Lib Dems who cheated on their expenses are not culpable either. But I'm afraid I think very little of rich Tories anyway and I expect them to be mean-spirited and grasping; after all, that's how rich people get rich, isn't it – by making sure that their own money is closely guarded and very little of it goes towards paying their staff extra or to benefit those less well-off than themselves.

What it really comes down to is your attitude towards people and how you see the rest of the world. If you expect the human race all to be selfish, out-for-themselves undeserving types, then that shapes the way you want your government to deal with them, by allowing you to hang on to as much of your own wealth as you can. This is why every time a Labour government looked like getting into power in the eighties and nineties, there was always a handful of rich celebrities who said they were going to leave the country. Never did, though, did they?

Not all wealthy people are tight-fisted misers though, to give them their due. Bill Gates, for example, seems to be single-handedly tackling the malaria problem in Africa with his money, and this harks back to the days of the Victorian philanthropists who used their money to benefit society (Hello, Margaret Thatcher), rather than just themselves and their families.

### 'What Has Feminism Ever Done For Me?'

Blimey, what a question. Where do you start? Well, first of all, if it hadn't been for the Suffragettes who were early feminists, Margaret Thatcher wouldn't even have had the vote or been able to get into Parliament. That courageous group of women put themselves through hell in order to win rights for women. It is ironic that had women *not* had the vote, the Labour Party would apparently have got in at almost every election in the last century. Mmm, a dilemma for left-wing women all over the country.

And feminists in the sixties allowed women to be freed up to work, use childcare and pursue their careers, rather than the no-choice scenario of staying at home and looking after their families which had been their lot for the preceding centuries. One might argue that feminism has just created the conditions for women to work twice as hard as before, by not only doing the bulk of the work domestically but also taking on work outside the home as well, but that is another issue.

I do think that women are in some ways the worst enemies of feminism, especially in the twenty-first century. Most young women have been scared off by the cartoon image of a feminist as a ball-breaking harridan who hates men, and it's going to be difficult to rid ourselves of the image that the right-wing press has tried so hard to create.

## 'The Lady's Not for Turning'

'You turn if you want to; the lady's *not* for turning.' Margaret Thatcher's famous play on words is lifted from the title of the play *The Lady's Not for Burning* by Christopher Fry. It was a response to calls from people to do a political U-turn and was seen by many as a positive character trait that she dug her heels in and forged ahead regardless. Ironically, she didn't know the play or understand the pun. Of course the speech had been written for her by someone else, so how would she know?

In my opinion, politics is about endless compromise and the ability to see the other person's point of view.

Margaret Thatcher was the Queen of Rigidity and in my book that is not a very attractive quality.

My main problem with Margaret Thatcher, apart from her being a dyed-in-the-wool Conservative, was the fact that she appeared to have no sense of humour. There were a number of occasions when she was called upon to do jokes in her speeches, and it was patently obvious that she didn't really know what she was saying. Famously, in one speech when she was supposed to say, 'As Moses said, keep taking the tablets,' I think she substituted the word 'pills', thus indicating that the joke that was staring her in the face had completely passed her by.

One of my favourite (reported) stories comes from when she was visiting a factory, and while moving through a group of young lads, remarked to one of them, 'That's an enormous tool you've got.' Much sniggering ensued . . . to Thatcher's complete bafflement.

## Tony Blair

I was not one of the bright young things who paraded round Downing Street at one of Tony Blair's famous parties when he got into power. Britpop was at its height and they allowed the famously unpredictable Gallagher brothers in, among others. I was still plugging away in

the background, doing benefits and rather unaccept-
ably later on supporting Ken Livingstone when he was
chucked out of the Party to stand as an Independent
for Mayor of London.

However, as time went on, I was called upon to go
to various events and say a few words in support of the
Party. I remember being at a rally in Hove just before
the 2005 election, as the seat there was under threat,
and found myself seated next to David Blunkett whom
I had not seen for many years. In fact, the last time I
had encountered him was at a MIND benefit up in
Scarborough, at which we were both due to speak. We
were in a room having a coffee and I was surreptitiously
smoking in the corner, in the days when smoking was
allowed in the corners of hotel rooms. David, of course,
is blind – and he shouted to the whole room, 'Who is
smoking in this room? I do not like it!'

So, I was forced to sidle up to him and admit my
guilt. Didn't get us off on a great footing: the teenager
versus the grown-up.

In Hove though, we were matier and he seemed
to have forgotten the smoking incident even if I
hadn't. I was sandwiched between David Blunkett
and Cherie Blair. Tony Blair came along the row,
shaking hands and saying hello, and he gave me a

kiss, with the words, 'Thanks so much for everything you're doing for us, Jo.'

I thought back to my schooldays, recalling how a few teachers in exasperation had told me I wouldn't amount to very much, and wished I could have had a photo taken to send to every one of those teachers, accompanied by the sound effect of a big raspberry. Just for the record, the Labour Party scraped in at Hove, so it might have done a minuscule bit of good.

Over the past few years leading up to the most recent election (2010) I have done more for the Labour Party than ever before, and have had to console myself with the fact that Labour lost less badly than they could have done. There have been a couple of Labour women's dinners that I have compered, and it has been very satisfying to perform to a room of left-wing women.

There is still a great lack of women in politics and I think it's important to do all we can to encourage women to go into this life, hard as it is. It is very important that our politicians reflect society as a whole and at the moment, gender-wise and race-wise, we can hardly say that they do.

The question arises then about whether you should artificially increase the number of women in Parliament by having women-only short-lists, when you are looking for a candidate to stand for the election. I am uneasy about doing this, but cannot think of a more effective way to up the proportion of women MPs.

Some years ago, I did a couple of events for something called Emily's List. This is an organisation that started up in America to support women candidates financially who were attempting to achieve a career in politics. The word Emily is an acronym for Early Money Is Like Yeast (it grows). Geddit? Sorry, America, but there is something quite yucky about that.

I hosted a dinner to raise money and found myself sitting on a table with some real Labour Party luminaries. I was sat next to Betty Boothroyd, who at the time was Speaker of the House of Commons. I half expected her, because that is the image I had of her, to start a singsong or give people great big comradely bear hugs. Interestingly though, I found her very reserved and quite difficult to talk to. Clare Short, on the other hand, said to me something like, 'I hope you're going to give them some shit.'

Barbara Castle was by that time in her eighties, yet she gave the most articulate, rousing and entertaining speech I had heard for years. She had always been a heroine of mine, and it is such a relief to meet one of your heroines and find them to be everything you hoped they would be.

Eventually, I was asked to an evening for Labour Party celebs to meet Tony Blair at a hotel near Downing Street. There too were Helen Worth (Gail from *Corrie*), Anthony Minghella, Steve Cram and Melvyn Bragg among others. I find these events a strange mix of fascinating and rather uncomfortable, and they make me want to ask, 'Why are we here?'

Tony Blair was only allotted so much time as he glided round saying hello and being charming to each of us. I found myself thinking, I must say something politically astute that he is a) impressed by and b) decides will become Labour Party policy. And then of course, as he got round to me, I just ended up saying, 'Oh hello, that's a nice tie,' or something similar.

I think that Tony Blair was probably the first child of the media-led politics generation. He was very astute and media-savvy, looked good in front of the camera, never seemed ruffled and always said the right thing. And that counts for a lot these days. Shallow though it may be, it seems to be what impresses the punters.

## Gordon Brown

Poor old Gordon Brown, on the other hand, does not easily do that media thing. As a person I admire him enormously, because I think his heart is in the right place. He has a strong sense of what is right democratically, and I believe genuinely wanted the best for the country and all the people who struggle with their lives. But something happens when you stick a camera in his gob that turns him into a different person. And these days people want their politicians looking like handsome estate agents in sharp suits. Gordon Brown, because of his rather hesitant manner and slightly strange mannerisms, was dismissed by a large number of the electorate as a bit of a weirdo.

However, all my meetings with him have shown him to be a warm, humorous, intelligent and dedicated person. I'm not convinced he's a bully, although I do reckon he's got a scary temper on him, but I haven't seen any evidence of that.

The first time I was due to meet Gordon Brown properly, I was at a charity event at Downing Street, but also due at a Labour Party dinner across Town that I had been asked to arrive at on time. As the minutes ticked on, several aide types came over and said to me and a couple of other comics, Lee Mack included, 'The Prime Minister will be over to meet you in a minute.'

Eventually it got too late, and when an aide came over for a third time and said it was going to be another five minutes, I had to say I couldn't wait. Lee Mack thought it was hugely amusing that I blew out the PM, but truth be told I was dying for a wee as well so I had to move. Oh, how the great moments in one's life are scuppered by the bladder.

I also did a couple of women-only fundraisers organised by Sarah Brown, who is as composed, quietly humorous and generous as she appears to be. These events were again to raise money, but also to encourage more women to get stuck into politics. Those attending were a mixture of women celebrities, prominent Labour Party women and a sprinkling of wealthy women.

To digress for a minute, at one such event I was compering, I sat next to a very rich woman who asked me whether I did birthday parties. In all honesty, I don't really like doing birthday parties because the guests all tend to know each other, and that changes the dynamic of the evening – since there is always the lurking possibility that they will turn on you as one. However, I did not immediately dismiss the idea, although as this woman was hugely glamorous, about twenty-two and absolutely dripping in squillions of pounds' worth of jewels, I couldn't imagine that an act such as mine would really fit in amongst the glitterati of Belgravia.

'Who did you have at your last birthday?' I enquired. 'Stevie Wonder,' came the answer. I gulped inside. My appearance at that woman's birthday party was never going to happen.

I was granted a private five-minute 'hello' sesh with Gordon Brown last time I did a women's fundraiser for his wife. In the room were me, Alesha Dixon and Gordon and Sarah, plus some security bods and the inevitable photographer. We had a relaxed chat and I marvelled that these moments were probably repeated endlessly throughout the lives of politicians and must be like a living hell.

At Christmas one year, Jack Dee and I did a show on Radio 2, and just as a laugh, I asked whether Gordon Brown would contribute a comedy line for it. To my surprise he agreed, and the producer and I went to Number Ten to record the line, which included a self-deprecating comment about being dour. After we'd done it, Gordon said he was off to a party for Labour supporters at a hotel in Central London and asked if I'd like to come with him. I said

I'd love to, and was then invited to travel there with him in his official car.

We were led down through the bowels of Downing Street, exiting at the rear straight into his waiting Jag. We both sat in the back, security men in cars at the front and behind, and flanked by outriders on bikes. It was one of the most exciting experiences, driving through the centre of Town extraordinarily fast, chatting to the PM and wanting to wind the window down and shout, 'Hey, look, everyone – it's me!' But I didn't, of course. Just sat there trying to look cool and behave as if I did that sort of thing all the time.

I found it really sad watching Gordon and Sarah Brown and their children leave 10 Downing Street. The election, if one could manage to be objective, was very interesting because, given how unpopular Gordon Brown was, one would have imagined that David Cameron would walk it.

However, I think people were suspicious of Cameron; he'd not had a very good press in terms of how posh he was, and his and Boris's link to the Bullingdon Club in which a load of over-privileged youths smashed up a restaurant and then paid for the damage, didn't show them in a very pleasant light. So where did the votes go, that Cameron didn't get? To Nick Clegg, who had suddenly acquired the status of a celebrity following the television debates? But no – the Lib Dems *lost* seats. They went, I presume, to cushion what could have been a much worse Labour defeat. So then the negotiations began, and to be honest, I never had any faith in the Lib Dems coming to any agreement with the Labour Party.

And so we were presented with a Tory/Lib Dem coalition. Will we have the harshness of the Tories, leavened with a bit of Lib Dem niceness? So they'll bring back hanging but they'll allow people a scented candle while they're being executed? I have to try not to think that we're being ruled by a bunch of Eton toffs or else I'd get too depressed. I predict the Lib Dems' input will get teenier and teenier until you can almost hardly notice it. Promises made before the election have already been broken, and I wonder how long it will take the British people to get sick of the draconian measures the Tories are taking to correct the deficit.

I don't think in politics that there are any definitive answers. For instance, who caused the global economic crisis in the first place?

It depends on who you vote for.

**Local Politricks**

And, of course, here in London we are being ruled yet again in a micro-way by the Tories, as a bunch of nanas voted Boris Johnson in as London Mayor for some reason. This floppy-haired, overgrown schoolboy was not my choice, and one can only hope that he puts his foot in it a few more times. He does occasionally seem like a young Duke of Edinburgh in the gaffe department.

But why did people vote for him?

People I know who did so, in the main, said they voted for him because he seemed like a laugh on *Have I Got News for You*. Well, so did Tom Baker – but I'm not sure I'd want him as Mayor of London. And Boris lives in North London, so he's obviously rubbish.

Celebrity-type exposure is encroaching more and more on politics these days. Politicians are on entertainment shows and celebs are going into politics. It's a rum old situation which, carried to its logical conclusion, may mean that (God forbid) Piers Morgan or Simon Cowell could end up running the country if we're not careful – in which case I would indeed emigrate.

# The Gender Agenda

### Do I Hate Men?

I'm often accused of hating men by the usual array of right-wingy tabloidy types who find it easy to slot me into that box so that they can hate me back.

It's interesting how, for thousands and thousands of years, in our society, men have had the upper hand – and as soon as women start to claw a bit of power into their lives, a number of men feel it's too much. Of course I don't hate men as an entire group – that would be utterly ridiculous, unless I was a separatist feminist lesbian, which I'm not.

I always used to do a line in my set in which I described the continuum along which feminism seems to run these days. At the one end it takes in what are called 'lipstick feminists' – women who have feminist ideals but want to do the whole feminine bit as well – right along to the other end where you find your male-clothes-wearing, short-haired, Doc Marten-sporting manhaters. The thing is that, emotionally, I am probably more up the end of the lipstick gals, but I look like I'm right down the other end with the dungaree-wearers.

The five top things men do that annoy me are:

1. *Consume pornography*
2. *Treat women like second-class citizens*
3. *Intimidate women when they are in groups*
4. *Good men tolerate bad men treating women like shit*
5. *The vast majority cannot help themselves equating good looks with attractiveness*

As a woman who has never – and will never – look like a model, one is constantly made aware of the level of one's attractiveness by those men who feel it's OK for them to randomly comment on a woman's position in the 'How-attractive-you-are-to-me-love' chart of female looks. Well, would you believe it, guys, quite a lot of us don't like that. And it's particularly galling, if you try to make a point about women being patronised, intimidated or not taken seriously, when the answer that comes back is: 'Oh, you're just jealous because you're ugly.'

This is *so* frustrating because I can hardly counter with, 'Oh come on, boys, look at me – I'm beautiful, admit it.' The interesting thing is that I know lots of really gorgeous-looking blonde women who are sick to bloody death of being treated as if they're thick as shit. And if you look at it, female types have, over the years, been divided into very clichéd groups to satisfy the easy categorisation of us lot.

So for example you have:

- The bimbo
- The slag
- The nympho
- The harridan
- The gold digger
- The frigid cow
- The lesbian (if you make it apparent you don't fancy them)

Ooh, how flattering it is, to hear one's gender divided into such positive categories. The division of men into categories like this does not seem to exist, but I wish it did. If I got the opportunity I would have:

- The woman loather
- The bed notcher
- The five-year-old child
- The 'I need a housekeeper' bloke
- The eternal band member
- The useless Herbert

I'm not saying that there aren't nice blokes around, there are plenty, but I'm sure men don't want to be reduced to a few pejorative phrases and neither do women.

Going back to the intimidation theme for a moment, here is a typical story. Recently I was in my car at the traffic-lights about midnight on the M11 link road and a young woman was in the car in front. A car containing two men drew up alongside her and the bloke on her side put down the window and began making the international sign for blowjobs at her. I was appalled and so angry. If I'd had a flamethrower in the car I would have used it. That sort of intimidation makes me so mad. I followed the two cars for a bit, in case they were going to do anything else, but thankfully a little further on, they turned off looking for pastures new.

It is incidents like this one and those from my own experience which continue to fuel the feminist principles I have – and that ain't never going to change. I really wish for more power for women to fight against this sort of bullshit, even though some people think that turns you into the anti-pleasure, anti-sex ball-breaking harridan described earlier in this book. Well, it doesn't, it just makes me want to even the balance and I suppose brings me back to the joke I did once about women being armed. If we women had the physical ability to look after ourselves, perhaps that would improve things a little.

As women's place in society seems at present to be regressing to what it was before the sixties and feminism happened, I have no idea what it's going to be like in the future. There are so many cultures impinging on ours that I believe have a dodgy attitude towards women, that it remains to be seen whether the end result will be a demotion of women's place in society and we'll end up back at home slogging our guts out domestically, being exploited and unable to put a foot outside the front door.

## Do I Love All Women?

No, of course I don't, because that would be as bloody ridiculous as hating all men. I find it really interesting these days that young women cannot bear to be associated with feminism and are embarrassed to be called a feminist, for the reasons stated on page 276.

The Spice Girls and 'girl power' made an attempt to improve things, but a group of young women who made pots of money aren't a very realistic role model for the rest of womanhood. In these days, when women can not only work but run a family as well, it seems to me that more and more responsibility is being heaped onto them and eventually they may just explode with the pressure.

However, that's not to say it's all bad. Changes are occurring.

In the days when I was a child, to be honest I hardly remember seeing my dad. He would disappear in the morning and then reappear in the evening just before we went to bed, and although he was around at the weekends and came on trips and holidays, he was quite distant compared to my mum. These days, dads are much more hands-on. The once exclusively female group who dropped children off for school has now opened up to include more than a smattering of men. One hopes that in this age of one step forward, two steps back gender relations, scores will eventually even between the sexes, and that some sort of parity will be achieved.

# THE BOX

# First Telly Tasting

Your first appearances on telly are so exciting because you can't quite believe you've wiggled your way into that flickering box that always sat in the corner of the living room throughout your childhood. Television has always been magical to me, and I can pretty much sit and watch any old bollocks from dawn till dusk. As a child I drew the line at The Budget, however, and used to be really pissed off when that was on because it meant they took *Crossroads* off the telly.

For those of you who don't remember *Crossroads* it was an early soap which revolved round a motel set outside Birmingham (oh, the glamour). Many people say that Victoria Wood based *Acorn Antiques* (the very,

very funny piss-take of a soap opera) on *Crossroads*, which was famous for its microphones in shot, scenery moving and enormously long pauses between the inter-action of some characters. My dad's friend from school, Ronald Allen, was in it playing David Hunter, and there were many memorable characters who just stayed in my head.

In my first year as a solo stand-up without the safety net of my psychiatric nursing job, I managed to make five appearances on TV and two of these were pilot shows. A pilot is a possible series which is given money to make just one show, see how it goes down with telly execs and the audience, and then it may be taken up and an entire series made. As you can imagine, hundreds of pilot shows fall at the first hurdle because the great idea in your head doesn't somehow translate into a workable piece of telly.

The two pilots I did both disappeared without trace. The first one was a sort of bohemian sketch show, the line-up being Hattie Hayridge (stand-up), Patrick Marber (stand-up, now writer), Vicki Lickorish (kids' telly), Paul Medford (actor), Josie Lawrence (actor, comedian) and James Macabre (stand-up). The show was a series of sketches, some music, and we went in every day for two weeks to a rehearsal room in Brixton, to work on it. We were a fairly diverse group and for some reason the show didn't work. Either it was because we were all so different, the chemistry wasn't there – or possibly just because the show was shit. Who knows?

It did not get commissioned, but in some ways this was probably a good thing as it set me down the road of reality. Decisions on what's going on the box and what isn't tend to ultimately be the decision of one person – and therefore come down to personal preference. To put it bluntly, if someone doesn't like you, you're out.

Then there is the problem of TV execs changing jobs every five minutes. You just manage to get something commissioned and then that person leaves and another one who can't stand you comes into the post. Or perhaps they simply want to stamp their own mark on the channel – in which case they clear out all the pending stuff and you are flushed down the toilet with all the other hopefuls.

The other show, for which I had much higher hopes but which also never went further than the 'possible' stage, was a comedy about a DSS snooper looking for people illegally claiming benefits. It revolved round a comedy club and starred Tom Watt (him off *EastEnders* who used to play Lofty and is now a sport radio pundit) and also Jerry Sadowitz, whom Tom was pursuing. The filming took place in Birmingham and was my first taste of what a pain it can be to film things like dramas. The problems are: it takes so long to set up cameras, get the sound right, have everyone in the right place, and make the audience behave normally i.e. not mouthing *Hello, Mum!* at the camera when it sweeps past. In fact, it all takes so long that eventually one starts to slip into a coma of boredom. I found the whole thing frustrating and irritating, which must be why I've never gravitated towards a career in drama and films. Oh all right then, I haven't 'cause I've always been pretty rubbish at acting.

Much of my early telly was just due to me saying, 'Oh God, yes please!' because I wanted to be on telly, thought if I turned it down they wouldn't ask again, and the money was pretty attractive too. That meant that I did make some pretty massive errors of judgement, not least a show called *Only Fools and Turkeys* in which I was a commentating Christmas fairy sitting in a café in West London. First of all I was dressed up as a fairy (looked bloody ridiculous, of course – and that was the point, I assume), then I was placed on a stool in a café by the counter to deliver a series of monologues to camera.

Well, I thought at least they might shut the café to make filming a bit easier, but oh no, they didn't bother.

So there I am sat on a stool, dressed as a fairy, looking like a twat, and just to add that extra frisson of joy, building workers are tramping in and out to get their bacon butties and making their feelings about the way I look perfectly clear. Christ, the humiliation. And as if that wasn't bad enough, I had assumed that the piece would be buried in the schedules around about teatime as it was a children's show and no comics would ever see it as they don't tend to get up till the news.

However, almost as soon as it had been transmitted, I got a call of the piss-taking variety from my friend Mark Lamarr, and realised I hadn't got away with it. I allowed him his victorious phone call and then thankfully it was never mentioned again.

I did quite a bit of TV with Mark, as I suppose at the time we were part of a group considered the hot young things. It has to be said he was much hotter than me as he was so young, barely twenty, whereas I was a bit lukewarm, being the grand old age of thirty.

At the time there was much socialising and staying up late, taking part in titanic drinking and card sessions. For a long time our card game of choice was called Black Maria, a very nasty affair which involved dumping the person next to you right in it. Of course, fuelled by drink, this was cause for much falling-out and rowing, but it all added to the fun of it.

I remember once when we had stayed up all night and Mark and I were due in Manchester early afternoon to do a TV show that night, which was a showcase for stand-ups. We realised we weren't going to be able to get any kip at all so, fuelled with a packet of ProPlus, the students' friend, we drove up to Manchester with the increasing ingestion of the aforementioned stimulant making us ever more wired and ever more grumpy. This may be the reason that I can't actually remember anything about the show at all, apart from the fact that Steve Coogan, John Hegley and Hattie Hayridge were in it. Not exactly the height of showbiz dissipation is it, ProPlus? At the time it was our only option apart from fifteen espressos.

These first TV appearances were a real learning curve. First of all, they were not like doing stand-up in a club. The audiences were more distracted because there was so much going on in the studio: cameras and cameramen/women moving about, the floor manager exhorting people to laugh/clap/cheer louder, and make-up people coming on constantly to add a layer of powder to the more sweaty ones amongst us. This made it difficult for the acts and the audience to really 'gel' and so a lot of the time one tended to feel one only had 70 per cent of their attention.

I found this difficult to get used to at the beginning, because it is easy to forget that actually your performance is for the *viewers*, so how you are doing with the audience is in many ways irrelevant. It's important to look straight down the barrel of the camera and give it everything you've got, regardless of the fact that the studio audience may be looking at you like they want you hung, drawn and quartered.

On these early occasions I came up against wardrobe people who wanted to change me from a lifelong scruff-bag into a middle-aged Tory matron. It was hard for me to be dressed up like a Christmas tree and decked out with sparkly accessories because I felt utterly ridiculous. As a woman who spends roughly 0.003 of a second on my hair and make-up in the morning, the idea of sitting in front of a mirror for up to half an hour while someone slapped God knows what on my face and hair was anathema to me. I just wanted to wear my scruffy black clothes and a slash of red lippie and go into battle with that, but instead I was battered, pummelled, waxed, had my hair pulled about, curled, straightened, moussed and sprayed – and by the time I tottered on stage I felt like a chubby tower of chemicals.

I eventually got used to this and have tried over the years to claw back a little bit of my own taste from the unrecognisable person who used to emerge from the make-up and wardrobe rooms. To be honest, if I ever catch a glimpse of my old TV appearances, I simply don't know myself.

One thing which was a help to me in my early telly career was being recalled to do more of *Friday Night Live*. (If I may blow my own trumpet very briefly here for one second, I was the only one.) This was a huge boost to my confidence and, I think, probably resulted in extra work starting to come in on TV and radio.

Other comedy and cabaret series I did at the time were *Up the Junction*, filmed at the Junction Folk Club in Cambridge and compered by Will Durst, a good solid political American comic who I liked, apart from the fact that at the end of the show he would say, 'You've been great, I've been Durst!' which made me very embarrassed for him because English audiences much preferred their comedy down-to-earth and non-showbizzy.

Also, I did a show in Soho a couple of times called

*Paramount City* which was a straightforward stand-up show compered by the delightful Arthur Smith. I have always thought of Arthur as the Sid James of alternative comedy owing to his rich London accent and craggy features.

In the early days I also did *Saturday Zoo*, on which Jonathan Ross was the presenter. Originally a researcher, he had been pushed forward from the bowels of the production office and he ran *Saturday Zoo* as if he was a natural.

I have always admired Jonathan Ross, given that again, like Russell Brand and Ricky Gervais, he came from an ordinary working-class background and didn't have an Oxbridge badge to smooth his passage into TV. He is very bright, has an eclectic knowledge and is charming and friendly. There is really only one thing about him that irritates me – and plenty of other people – and that is his attitude towards attractive women on his radio and television show, which can be patronising beyond belief!

When I'm watching or listening, I see it as an unavoidable trial to get through, as he regales each female guest with honeyed words about how gorgeous they look – at which a sizeable proportion of the female population, judging from the straw poll I've done, feel like they want to vomit and consider reaching for the off button. I can't think why, but he doesn't do this to me and treats me as an equal. I know some women are flattered by this kind of quasi-pervy admiration, but I bet there are a few who smile and accept his compliments through gritted teeth and wish he'd move on from treating them like they're a tasty morsel to be eaten with the eyes.

Over the years, women who resent being assessed on their appearance have been categorised as unattractive, resentful old harridans who are envious of other women's beauty. To anyone who thinks this, I would say, 'Grow up,' and incidentally I have the same attitude towards women who like certain footballers because they look nice or have sexy legs. I find this equally patronising and this attempt by women to equal the score by objectifying men strikes me as silly.

This was the point in my career when I began to meet proper grown-up stars. I remember having a coffee outside the production office once and wondering what a little girl was doing there. The little girl in question was facing away from me and appeared to be wearing quite adult clothes. Then she turned round and it was Kylie Minogue. I could not believe what a tiny little perfectly formed person she was, and being introduced to her I felt like a giantess with sausagey fingers and a socially unacceptable bulk – which is exactly the line many of the tabloids took when I started to appear on telly.

One of my less happy memories of TV was *The James Whale Show*. James Whale was a controversialist whose *raison d'être* appeared to be to slag everyone off. His show was a mix of interviews, chat and music with regular guests. Jim Miller and I were booked to do a song, so we did a pastiche of a song called 'Summer the First Time', a romantic song about the first sexual encounter between a young man and an older woman. Of course we had comedied it up and filthied it up. One of the guests on the show was DJ Mike Read, who had been responsible for banning Frankie Goes To Hollywood's slightly rude single 'Relax' from the airwaves, so he sat through our song with a stony expression on his face looking like he'd sucked a lemon. And at the end of the song, just to land ourselves in it even more, I announced, 'Oh, look! There's James Whale's wife over there grazing.'

I hadn't realised that James's wife really *was* at the show and probably wouldn't have done it if I'd known. James Whale was furious, but it was not an attack on his wife – it was an attack on *him*. I have always felt that if you dish it out big time, you have certainly got to be able to take it.

I found myself in a similar position when I was on *Wogan*, the telly show, with David Sullivan, the newspaper porny man. As is so often the case when one meets people of his nature – well, what do I mean by that? What I mean is that he seemed like a perfectly pleasant bloke.

But I have a problem with the porn industry, and however much people may argue that . . .

- It's just a bit of fun.

- The women in it earn a packet (as opposed to putting their mouths round one).

- The women have control.

. . . none of this balances the fact that . . .

- The image projected of women in porn is not a 'bit of fun' for the readers who absorb it and use it to justify treating women with contempt.

- Only the top porn stars 'earn a packet'. The rest are exploited and desperate, and if you have ever watched cheap porn, you can see that. They are either thin as sticks, look stoned or look like robots.

- Again, only the elite few have control; the rest grin and 'bare' it.

So despite Mr Sullivan's surface charm, I felt I could not just sit back on a sofa with him and nod sagely as if I agreed with his existence. So, I felt it my duty to have a go and banged out some jokes about the size of his tackle and generally tried to take the piss out of him. All right, I accept it wasn't the most sophisticated attack, but I was obviously not there to outline the academic feminist argument in its fullest sense, I was there to do comedy and that's what I tried to do.

## Sister Frances

*Sister Frances* is a sitcom that never was, a funny (I thought) show about nuns that sadly didn't ever make it past the pilot.

As I mentioned earlier, pilots demonstrate the approach TV companies take to new comedy. They are able to get an idea of how the show will be without having to actually commit themselves to a series. They make pilot shows basically because they like the idea but are a bit worried that the transition from the initial idea and script will result in the programme being crap – and fair dos, it can happen.

I wrote *Sister Frances* with a comedy writer called Sue Teddern who was coming at it from a very different angle to me. Her approach was more traditional, I suppose, whereas I constantly have to rein myself in or else the result would be so dark, people probably couldn't cope with it. This was before *Nighty Night* and the like.

We negotiated with ITV who said they wanted something for the late evening, post watershed. So that was what we did – quite rude, quite dark. Having produced this, they then changed their minds and said it should be more whimsical and quirky and suitable for 7.30. So out came a fair bit of filth and some of the darker moments, which was a shame as my comedy is much more suited to late night.

I find writing stuff and the process of refining it pretty exhausting. Once I've written something, I can't see the point of constantly going back to it because I always think that makes it worse. Still, we hacked away at it, Sue saying things to me like, 'You can't have a dead nun in a cupboard,' and me saying things to her like, 'Why do Terry and June have to come in at this point?' For all our differences, we got on well and finally came up with something we were happy with.

We got a cast together including my lovely friend Morwenna Banks who is very funny indeed, and Honor Blackman who used to be in *The Avengers* and agreed to be the Mother Superior. *Sister Frances* was filmed in a studio with an audience and of course, although you have rehearsed it endlessly, it's always quite a scary experience to get your first audience sitting in front of it.

Sadly, it didn't go brilliantly – I thought because we'd had to cut some of the more grown-up stuff. I found myself at one point, dressed as a nun, in Mother Superior's office with some exercise equipment, thinking, Oh bollocks, this isn't working at all.

*Sister Frances* was not commissioned in the end because the channel felt it was too tame for a time slot of 10.30 p.m. Well, that was the first we'd heard of it going back to its original late slot, and I was bloody frustrated about this because I would have beefed it up big time, had I thought we could get away with a lot more.

So, we all moved on, but I was well pissed off about it because it seems we couldn't even communicate between ourselves what time of night the bloody thing should be on.

Oh well, thank the Lord for *Through the Cakehole*.

# Through the Cakehole
# with My Cakehole

*Through the Cakehole* was a comedy series with sketches and stand-up that I did for Channel Four, and which I think I got on the strength of me staggering onto the stage at Edinburgh a couple of times. I did the show through a production company called Channel X which was part-owned by Jonathan Ross and a couple of other telly types (who were very normal and nice for telly types) called Katie Lander and Mike Bolland.

I wrote the series with my friend Jim Miller and the enormity of it only struck us when we started doing it. Filling six half-hours of comedy is not easy. We wanted to have a long-running serial within it, so we came up with *Drudge Squad*, which to this day is my favourite thing I've done on telly.

*Drudge Squad* was supposed to portray the life of a woman with a slightly useless husband as she attempted to juggle her job as a police detective and her role as a mother. My sidekick was played by my friend Maria McErlane.

*Drudge Squad* centred round the minutiae of a mother's life, like nappies hanging up to dry in the back of police cars, the main characters turning up late owing to crises at home, and various items of domestic apparatus being used to handcuff prisoners.

We managed to get a few car chases in, which I'd really wanted to do, and did a lot of the filming on a rather scary estate in Acton, just hoping we wouldn't be surrounded by a gang who nicked our cameras and all our worldly goods.

I think my favourite day on *Drudge Squad* was the day we managed to drive a car into the sea. I have no idea why the production team agreed to fork out the money for this, as it must have cost a bloody fortune. In the car were myself, Maria and Simon Clayton who played my husband Dave. We were in a battered Ford which had a chain attached to the back of it to drag us out in case it all went horribly wrong and we all started drowning. Maria and I were extremely excited and looking forward to it, whereas poor old Simon obviously thought it was all going to go pear-shaped and looked slightly sweaty and terrified.

We drove down a sort of concrete ramp and in we went to a pretty millpond-ish sea. We got in pretty deep and the car began to sink as we desperately tried to deliver our lines in a reasonably professional way. Before we could actually drown we managed to get out of the car and wade back chest-deep in waves, still delivering lines. The car was dragged out by the chain and back onto the slipway. There had been some camera or sound problem so the director asked for another take. Mmm – wet car, no chance. Amazingly, the car started first time when I turned the key in the ignition and in we went again, Simon not best pleased at having to reprise his performance.

The rest of the show was a collection of higgledy-piggledy sketches. Among my favourites were:

**The Bernard Manning Sketch**
In this sketch we populated an entire country village with black people and I, as the only white person, drove through it as a series of black faces looked with

shock at me. Being a typical English village it looked completely surreal. The punch line to the sketch occurred when I walked into the local pub, again populated only by black people, and marched up to the bar taking down the hood on my coat as I did so. The barman looked at me and said, 'Oh thank God, we thought you were Bernard Manning.' Tense atmosphere then changes into a party one.

## Fat People Sketch

Four of us, me, Ricky Grover, JoJo Smith and 'The Man with the Beard', stand-up Kevin McCarthy, were stuffed into the tiniest Fiat imaginable and just drove round looking for eating opportunities. We took over an ice-cream van and were just allowed to do what we wanted. I'm not sure the sketch came out particularly funny, but the four of us had such a good laugh doing it, and I would like to thank Channel X for their indulgence in allowing us to get away with it.

## The Gold Blend Coffee Couple Piss-Take

This was a sketch I did with actor Kevin McNally who went on to greater things like *The Pirates of the Caribbean*. This was the slobs' version of the romance between the golden pair via instant coffee.

I knocked on a door looking shit wanting to borrow some coffee and it was answered by Kevin, unshaven, in his pants and looking god-awful. At this point an exchange followed between us which mined the depths of filth and double entendre around the topic of tea bags and coffee.

This was perhaps the most difficult sketch I've done in terms of trying to keep a straight face. Kevin looked so brilliantly awful and pervy that every time I opened the door, I just could not hold back my laughter. After several takes I realised I was really irritating everyone, but unfortunately that only made me worse. Suffice to say it went on for ever and I did eventually get bored with laughing.

Other sketches included actors Helena Bonham Carter, Craig Ferguson, Gary Webster off *Minder* and Martin Kemp, former heart-throb from Spandau Ballet. I was very impressed that any of these guys were happy to do a daft sketch show with an unknown comedian in it, and I found them all charming, unstarry and easy to work with. I know you'd like me to say they were a pain in the arse and demanding. But they weren't.

We did two series of *Through the Cakehole* and I found it very hard. The main problem being that by the time a channel has decided that they actually want a series, the time available to write it has shrunk to virtually nothing – maybe a few weeks. At one point Jim and I rented a house in Suffolk for a week to force ourselves away from the local joys of pub quizzes, friends and general entertainment. But there is something about being holed up together when you have to write comedy under duress that makes any potential comedy ideas just leak out of your head. It was a fractious time and after a few days we were both on the point of what your tabloid newspaper would call 'a breakdown'. We had cabin fever, couldn't think of anything funny, rowed and felt a bit helpless.

Rescue came in the shape of our mate Jeff Green who came for a visit and lifted the highly charged atmosphere. Everyone calmed down and the work started again, although we did stop in the evening to have drinks and play Scrabble. There had, I felt, been a slightly weird atmosphere in the cottage where we were staying, and one night as Jeff and I picked out letters for Scrabble, I got consecutively E V I L. Well, it was shaping up to be the opening of a horror film. I then picked three anonymous vowels. Jeff picked his letters. The first three were E V I . . . My heart skipped a beat and I held my breath . . . An M appeared. We all had a good laugh and told ourselves retrospectively that we knew we were being ridiculous.

The series got written, as did the next one, in a completely random and chaotic way. I suspect the general public may have visions of comedians sitting in some luxurious office surrounded by lackeys supplying coffees and any other requirements, but in my case it was late-night sessions with a notebook, a bottle of brandy, smoking my head off and watching some crappy late-night programme about students trying to cook.

# Getting On with It

*Getting On* is a series about nurses looking after the elderly in the NHS. I have already written a little about it in the chapter called *A Day in My Life*. I had always wanted to do a comedy that could also make people sad as well as laugh, and as there are so few programmes with old people and middle-aged women in them, I really wanted to go down that road.

My friend Vicki Pepperdine lives just down the road from me and had done some great comedy stuff like *The Hudson and Pepperdine Show* on Radio 4. In fact, I met her because she used to live next door to my best friend Betty and we'd chatted over the wall a few times. We punted some ideas to the BBC, none of which were received with anything other than indifference, so one day we sat around brainstorming ideas for shows which would contain a few old bags (ourselves) and we also got Jo Scanlan in too. She was a friend of Vicki's and they worked together on a fantastic comedy called *Coming Soon* on Channel Four, which was about a theatre group touring Scotland. It also starred David Walliams and Ben Miller, and was so funny I couldn't believe it when it finished prematurely and didn't appear again. Jo is also in *The Thick of It*, the incomparable political comedy from Armando Iannucci.

We felt that although the NHS had been done to death in comedy form, there was still room for a realistic, downbeat comedy which tried to remain faithful to the way the Health Service is these days, so we got together a proposal for the series and contacted a production company called Vera, with whom I'd made *Through the Cakehole* 800 years ago. We had one of those lunchtime meetings that people in telly have and which in some ways is just an excuse to have lunch and one wonders if anything is really going to come out of it. However, the MD Geoff Atkinson, who is a lovely person, was very keen and so we thought we'd move it on to the next stage.

A meeting was arranged with Janice Hadlow, who at

the time was the Controller of BBC4. (Have I said I love that word 'controller' – it's so *1984*, isn't it, and makes me think of Thomas the Tank Engine's Fat Controller. Before I read the books to my daughters, I always had the emphasis wrong and thought he controlled fat, rather than being a Controller who happened to be fat.)

As luck would have it, BBC4 were doing a season on the elderly and Janice thought that *Getting On* would fit very well into that season. After some discussion, they finally let us know that they were happy to commission three episodes and see how it went. I was ecstatic. This was something I really wanted to do, so we set about getting a loose script together, around which we could improvise and see how it went.

I have to apologise to Jo and Vicki at this point, but I had so much other work on, I left them to do a fair bit of the donkey work sketching the ideas into script form. Many of the areas we covered were things that had happened to me as a nurse or in hospitals, and so we decided to kick off the series with having an un-identified poo on a chair and the rigmarole that now surrounds sorting it out bureaucratically.

We were so pleased that Peter Capaldi had agreed to direct it because we thought he would give it that realistic feel that we were after. If I'd been after glamour, I wasn't going to find it on *Getting On*. I played Kim Wilde, a put-upon, knackered, slap-dash middle-aged nurse returning to nursing after having had children. Incidentally I realised this is the name of a well-known pop singer. I mentioned it to her when we worked on a Christmas show. She said she'd be happy to appear as a patient! Vicki played Dr Moore, a snooty, hypocritical and ambitious doctor, stuck in a backwater hospital and desperate to progress in her career. Jo was Sister Den Flixter, capricious, lazy and longing for love. And of course we had the gorgeous Ricky Grover playing Hilary Loftus the nurse manager – pompous, spouting psychobabble and unsure of his sexuality.

Having got loose scripts together, we finally moved towards filming. We had hired a hospital ward in the Bolingbrooke in Wandsworth and all met at seven on a Monday morning, cold and shattered, ready for filming.

The cliché that filming is glamorous is completely wrong. Mostly you have to start so early that you've had no sleep the night before and you look and feel shit. As we were actually in a hospital there was none of the Winnebago bollocks for us; we were in a small office with some nice hospital armchairs. In fact, the only thing that was perfect was the food. Breakfasts totalling roughly 15,000 calories were provided so that by the end of a three-week shoot it was perfectly feasible that you would have put on 27 stone. Added to this, at lunchtimes there were real proper puddings like treacle tart and jam roly-poly, and it's always bloody difficult to run away from them. Add on top sweets-agogo available all over the set, and bugger the Winnebago, we had everything we needed.

We got our uniforms on and I looked in the mirror with the bare minimum of make-up on and thought, God, that's horrendous. However, I was supposed to be a middle-aged, exhausted nurse in the NHS so I could hardly justify having a make-up person attempt to help me look my best. (Although this doesn't seem to stop them in *Holby City*.)

On the set we also had lots of what I used to call extras, but are now called supporting artistes – which sounds a bit posher. They were the most delightful group of women in their sixties and seventies, of whom I became incredibly fond over the three weeks we filmed. Their job would normally be to wander past in the background on *EastEnders* or *Harry Potter*, but we asked a little bit more of them – and that was to improvise with us in scenes. They didn't actually have to learn lines but just throw out the odd sentence which matched their character and illness – and they were brilliant at it. It looked very natural and non-forced, and the lucky buggers got to lie in bed all day.

We would film the same scene three or four times based round the script and plot, and as we refilmed we would add ideas as they came to us and so build on what we had already filmed. This meant that when it came to the editing process there was bloody loads of stuff for Peter and the others to wade through. I was just glad it wasn't down to me to decide.

I got so used to the ward and became very happy with parking my arse at the nurses' station and 'looking at the computer'. What was actually happening was that I had found a game of Solitaire on the computer and became slightly obsessed with it, to the detriment of my concentration.

We did have a huge laugh. Ricky particularly has a talent for making you helpless with laughter during a scene, and being the most unprofessional of the three of us, I'm sure there were a few scenes where I look like I'm going to explode, given that I'm trying so hard not to laugh.

The three weeks passed very quickly and then the three episodes were edited. We used a lovely song by the Sheffield singer Richard Hawley as the theme tune. It is called 'Roll River Roll', and it created the perfect atmosphere for the show.

When *Getting On* was broadcast we all held our breath. I never have any confidence in my own performance and wondered whether critics would say Jo and Vicki were great but I was complete shite.

To our delight, the critics were universally positive and well over the top in some cases. The viewing figures were fantastic and I remember getting a text from Ricky Grover (expletives deleted) remarking on how weird it felt to be in something successful.

I felt this strongly too. Over the years, I have clung on by my fingertips, presuming that at some point I would go right off the radar, return to touring and then disappear from view. So to be involved in a series like this which has sent my career in another direction is very gratifying.

Jo and I were nominated for a BAFTA for our performances in *Getting On*, and were miffed that Vicki didn't get a nod too. As it panned out, the BAFTA was won by Rebecca Front from *The Thick of It*. I was just pleased to even be nominated in the area of acting. It still makes me laugh when I think of it. What a hoot!

# Trinny and Susannah –
# The Scary Sisters

Trinny and Susannah's show *What Not To Wear* was a popular programme on the BBC in which they grabbed members of the public, had a right go at them about the way they were dressed, pummelled them emotionally and physically, humiliated them by making them take off most of their clothes and then stand in front of a 365-degree mirror, and then set about turning them into a new person.

There were a couple of specials made and I was invited to do a show called *Trinny and Susannah on the Red Carpet*. The purpose of this was to do what they did, except with celebrities, and the finite point of the show was then to push us up the red carpet in front of the paparazzi to present an award at the BAFTAs, done up in our finery.

I and Sophie Raworth, a BBC news presenter, were called upon to do the honours.

Our initial contact involved a meeting at some rich bloke's penthouse in Battersea that he let out for filming purposes. I was sat down between Trinny and Susannah on a luxurious sofa, at which point they turned on the telly and showed me a DVD of my fashion faux pas. To be honest, I wasn't that bothered by what they said. I thought I looked OK in all my so-called hideous incarnations, which is obviously my problem! OK, my hair looked bloody ridiculous in the eighties, but whose didn't? They also commented that I looked and dressed like a man. So what? Couldn't give a toss, quite honestly. Yes, I wore black baggy clothes, but that was down to laziness and shunning white for fear of looking like a marquee. I am and always have been a closet Goth, and also black has the advantage of shaving off a couple of pounds – and I'm not going to pass up that opportunity.

They stuck me in front of the infamous mirror, luckily not just in my bra and pants but with some tight black things on. But I wasn't even bothered about that really.

It wasn't a surprise for me nor, I would imagine, for the viewers either.

We then set about finding something for me to wear and so I was taken shopping to fat lady departments in posh stores round London. Trinny had a good old go (when I came out of a changing room), at pulling my knickers down, I can't really remember why now, but a small battle developed, which I easily won because even though she's tough as old boots, it appears I'm tougher.

I was also dragged to the office of a designer – a woman called Anna Scholz. She has tried to make clothes for big women which are a little more imaginative and glamorous. That's fine for the big women who want to be glamorous, but I don't. However, I went along with it because I was interested in which role model they would cast me as. Would it be Widdecombe? I feared the worst.

On the whole I quite enjoyed myself, had a pop at them when I could, and steeled myself for what I assumed would be some sort of unexpected, further attempt at humiliation. It eventually arrived one morning in the Battersea penthouse when the production team informed me they just wanted to 'do something' and sat me in a sort of dentist's chair under a very bright light, with a camera running, but refused to say why.

At this point, Susannah, who seemed to have been cast as the good copper (i.e. to persuade the criminal – me – to do or say something I didn't want to), appeared with a pair of tweezers and announced to the camera that she was going to deal with the hair-growth on my chin.

The moment had come, then. I felt this was a deliberate attempt to humiliate me over something which isn't a big deal (I hardly had a Brian Blessed beard at the time), but which women are made to feel embarrassed about – excess hair-growth. I was particularly pissed off, because they hadn't checked it out with me first – presumably because they thought, quite correctly, that I wouldn't agree to it.

I began to get angry, at which point Susannah panicked a bit and said, 'It's a problem we've all got, you know, Jo,' and attempted to turn the tweezers on herself. I bundled her out of the way and launched into a speech right down the barrel of the camera, about how the subtext of their show was about making women feel bad – and embarrassing and humiliating them. I stated that I didn't care, because I could stand up for myself and I knew all about attempts of producers to make 'good telly' and I wasn't having it – but, I went on to say, most women on that show weren't as experienced as I was and under the glare of the camera, nervous and malleable, they agreed to things that I thought were exploitative and unkind.

I continued with my rhetoric, at which point they wheeled out the producer, who asked the most brilliant question a producer has ever asked me. She said, 'Would you like to have a lie-down?'

My answer was something along the lines of, 'Are you having a laugh? No, I *don't* want a lie-down. I am not tired, elderly, disabled or ill. And of course you're implying that I am somehow being histrionic, because I'm what you sneeringly call "The Talent". I DO NOT WANT A LIE-DOWN!'

I peppered all this with a few more expletives and there was a bit of a stand-off. It took a while for the atmosphere to cool back down to normal and then we carried on. However, this is a very good example of how some television-makers handle people really badly.

We then continued as if nothing had happened, although they seemed a bit wary from that point on. Fine by me. As for the director who'd said earlier on, 'We need a bit more conflict,' he certainly got what he wanted.

Eventually, T and S got an outfit together for me

which included their requirements of a bit of cleavage (yuk) and emphasising a waist, which in all honesty I didn't really possess, particularly as I'd had a baby relatively recently. On the night of the BAFTAs, I was put into the outfit, a brown Anna Scholz two-piece consisting of a long skirt, top and velvet coat with leopardskin lining, which was perfectly all right but not really me. I was made up to within an inch of my life and then driven to the bottom of the red carpet to face the phalanx of paps waiting for blood.

God, it was hideous, the worst bit of the whole show, and I was so relieved when I got inside. I then had to present an award, can't even remember what for now, with the athlete Denise Lewis. (Yes, a comedy Laurel and Hardy thing going on there, I'm sure.)

I was so happy to get home that night, peel off my grown-up lady outfit and put on the familiar, black baggy, food-stained clothes in which I felt like myself. That outfit was given to me as a present at the end of filming and I haven't worn it since.

I have seen Trinny and Susannah a few times over the years and they are actually all right, although you may not be surprised to learn that we're not new best friends. They, like everyone else, just got sucked into the maelstrom of the ever voracious God of Good Telly.

# Wonderful Whiteley

*Countdown* has been one of my favourite things to do *ever* over the years. Firstly, because I was so familiar with it and watched it from the kick-off. It started in November 1982 on Channel Four. I had just left university and begun work as a nurse in the Emergency Clinic in South London, and whenever I was on early shift I would arrive home knackered and put it on. I was always tired after early shifts which started at seven, because however hard I tried I could not go to bed at a sensible time so I would rise at 6.15 having had about five hours and sometimes even less than that.

At that time I was living in a tiny little bedsit-type flat on Denmark Hill. There wasn't even enough room for a bed so I had a bed-settee thing which I would laboriously have to turn from one to another twice a day. Sometimes in the mornings I didn't even bother. I would get home from work and just go back to bed like an exhausted slug, barely managing to raise myself, apart from toilet and tea. It was ground floor and I suppose I should have felt slightly security-conscious, but I never did.

More fool me, because once when I was in hospital I got burgled and, paranoid that I am, I always imagined that somehow the burglars had a hotline to the hospital computer and burgled homes of patients because they knew they weren't at home.

The reason why I was in hospital was an allergic reaction to some hair colour. I used to dye my hair different shades when I got bored with it, and this time round it was a reddish dye rather ironically named 'Nice 'n Easy'. The reaction was my fault because I didn't do what is called a 'patch test'. This involves putting a tiny bit of the dye on your skin and then waiting a while to see if there is some reaction. Well, I have no patience whatsoever so I couldn't be bothered. Patch tests are for wimps! I had used hair colour before and assumed it would be OK. What I didn't know was that an allergic reaction can come out of nowhere even if you haven't had one before. So I put the dye on, left it for forty minutes as instructed and then went to bed. Almost immediately my head started to hurt and after an hour it was (pardon me for this description) leaking copious amounts of pus and really hurt. I rinsed my head under the cold tap, took some painkillers and went to sleep.

When I woke up in the morning, my face felt a bit weird and on looking in the mirror, I didn't recognise the Far Eastern woman of about seventy who was looking back at me. My eyes were so puffy I could barely see through them, and so I wondered whether I should take myself off to A&E. But being also slightly allergic to hospitals, I just put on a pair of sunglasses and headed out to meet some friends.

When I arrived, their reaction was enough to tell me that things were bad and they persuaded me to go to hospital. There I was given some drugs to sort it and left quite happily. The next day I still looked like Madam Bloaty Face and I felt worse. So back I went to the hospital with two friends, Jim and Andy. The nurses looked at them as though they'd given me a beating, and I was immediately admitted and put on intravenous steroids. By this time I couldn't see a bloody thing and soon found myself in a ward of elderly ladies. The poor old woman opposite me just kept shouting, 'Please, someone kill me!' Apparently, she couldn't see either and was in the last stages of cancer. It was very depressing and sad, and added another positive in my head towards the case of euthanasia.

A few friends visited and sniggered at the end of the bed, and it took a whole week before I was back to normal. And halfway through this week, the burglary happened. I was called by the police in hospital and had to go home and survey the damage. I think I quite frightened the police with my puffy moon face. Still, I had some time off and got to watch more *Countdown*s.

My dad loved *Countdown* too and at one point even auditioned for it. Unfortunately I don't think he ever got more than five-letter words and was unceremoniously informed that he would not be in the show.

As time went on, I was eventually asked whether I would come and be in Dictionary Corner and I was dead chuffed to be asked. *Countdown* was filmed at Yorkshire TV studios in Leeds and the day involved leaving home at about 5.30 in the morning, catching the 6.50 train from King's Cross, arriving at Leeds at 10-ish and then rushing over to the studio, into make-up to be ready on camera at 10.30. We would do two shows in the morning and three in the afternoon, then come back on the 7 p.m. train and be home by about 10.30 – a bloody long day. Vivienne, my agent, always came with me and we viewed it as a bit of a day out.

The first host of *Countdown* was the inimitable Richard Whiteley, an interesting mixture of a man with elements of your grandad, an Oxford don and an old-fashioned ladies' man.

I became terribly fond of him. He had that sort of 1950s sense of humour which consisted of terrible puns laced with gentle jokes. He was perfect for *Countdown*. Older viewers could giggle along with his puns, which had a warm familiarity about them and students – the other big group of viewers – could take the piss in an affectionate way.

Richard was always so friendly and welcoming, as were the production team, like a little family who have been together for years. This is unusual in television, as it's mainly young, thrusting and tends to have a lot of people called Jake and Sophie working in it.

I always used to sit in Dictionary Corner with Susie Dent and we would have sweets hidden under our desk, the consumption of which had to be very carefully timed so you weren't caught on camera chewing like a Friesian. Susie and I would pass notes to each other during the show, discussing the relative merits of various showbiz men we'd met and who we'd snogged. It was very good fun.

The scandal of the earpiece erupted on *Countdown* some years ago. One of the papers revealed that guests were fed words through an earpiece just in case they were thick as shit and couldn't come up with anything longer than three letters. I never considered this a big deal particularly. A sizeable majority of the production team were ex-*Countdown* champions, and it stands to reason that they would come up with something interesting. And who wants to hear someone like me say, 'Yes, I've got a six too.'

After a while I developed a little game in Dictionary Corner which involved me making up my own words. This has become somewhat of an albatross round my neck as now it means I *have* to do it. My favourite word to date is 'Cronenav' – a satnav system where an old lady sits in the back of your car and tells you where to go.

I was very upset when Richard died; he left a big hole in a lot of people's lives. The last time I saw him, we were on something called *Starspell* together, a celebrity spelling competition. He and I found ourselves in the final two. I am a right fascist about spelling and very competitive, so I really wanted to win. As it drew nearer to the climax, I got the word 'philately' which I knew well, but because I stumbled, I was disqualified and Richard won, but I found myself not minding at all because he was so lovable. Incidentally, during that show is the only time my pants have fallen down on telly. The pair I had on were too small and kind of rolled themselves down. Thankfully I was wearing trousers so they only got as far as my knees so it could have been a lot worse.

Richard was replaced by Des Lynam and then Des O'Connor, whom I knew vaguely, having filled in on his chat show *Des and Mel*. Des is a real giggler and a sweet bloke, and one day when I was feeling dead rough at *Countdown*, he turned up at my dressing-room door holding a bottle of Jim Beam. That was an interesting recording.

After the two Deses came Jeff Stelling, who I don't feel I know at all, yet. I have only done *Countdown* once under his benign gaze, so an opinion has not been formed, but *Countdown* has been one of the great pleasures of my life both as a viewer and a participant.

# Panel Beating

Panel shows are comedian fodder and they all have a fair sprinkling of the country's hot new comics on them, as well as some old lags like me.

The most successful panel shows to date have been, I think, *Have I Got News For You*, *They Think It's All Over* and *QI*.

I first did *Have I Got News* early in the nineties, and I was bloody terrified. Angus Deayton was still the host and Paul Merton and Ian Hislop, as they are now, were so confident, on the ball and funny that it was a daunting prospect for a relatively inexperienced stand-up such as myself. I was also aware that an appearance by a woman on these shows was as rare as an empty doctor's surgery, so I did feel the weight of expectation upon me and that just increased my anxiety. On my first show I was so grateful to Fred Macaulay, a lovely Scottish comic who was doing the warm-up. He was very encouraging and supportive, telling me not to worry and giving me a few suggestions for lines pertaining to the week's news and I will be eternally grateful to him.

However, once the lights go up, you are always on your own. As someone who is used to being cooperative and doing a lot of 'No, after you', I found it hard to force my way in and spout out possibly fall-flat-on-their-arse jokes – still do, in fact. And there is nothing worse than throwing out a line you think will really make 'em laugh, only to be greeted with stony-faced indifference. Fred Macaulay used to have a lovely line for when that happened and would say, 'That's the best that joke has ever gone.' Would have loved to have nicked that off him, but have made it a rule that I don't steal anyone's material.

Sometimes when you watch *HIGNFY* you think, Blimey, that guest hardly said anything. I always feel for those people because I know how hard it can be to make your mark on a show whose permanent members are so brimming with talent and confidence.

After I'd done a few shows, I stopped for a while as I just didn't seem to have the butting-in and delivering-a-killer-line skill, and when you think you're being crap at something, my advice is to try harder for a bit and then if it still doesn't work, stop doing it. Surely it's better not to be on something, than be crap on it.

Recently I have started guest-hosting *HIGNFY* which I find much more enjoyable. Being in that chair gives you an authority that I just didn't feel I had when I was a guest on the panel. It's not only about having funny lines, it's about having the confidence to deliver them, and even the funniest joke in the history of the universe, delivered hesitantly, will not go as well as a bad joke delivered with your big guns.

This, I think, is a real case in point as far as *Mock the Week* is concerned. I keep being told by people that I have slagged off *Mock the Week*, but I don't think I have. I have just been truthful about how I find it when I'm on it.

Much of a programme's character is down to the producer, and *Mock the Week*'s producer is called Dan Patterson, an experienced, talented and nice bloke. His production company is called 'Angst' and for good reason. He is very tight and quite controlling about what he wants, and I found that a difficult framework to work within. Besides that, there are seven comedians in it, all vying for attention on MTW, and I found myself thinking, Can I really be arsed to fight for airtime with all these guys who are so keen, confident and funny? And the answer that came back to me was, 'No, I can't,' so I stopped doing the show, simple as that. It doesn't suit me and that's all there is to it.

*They Think It's All Over* by its very nature was predominantly male, testosterone-fuelled and not a place for the shrinking violet to be residing. Nick Hancock is a mate of mine so I'm ashamed to say I treated it partially as a social event where I could catch up and have a natter with him. I found Gary Lineker a good laugh to work with, and we would always find something to have a bet on, whether it was a challenge to get a particular word in or to answer a particular question.

I once answered a question about football and politics that involved Germany acknowledging the Independence of Croatia. Gary simply refused to believe that I had not been given the answer before the show, but I hadn't. I do read the papers. Maybe he thought I sat at home poring over *Heat* magazine. Well, I do, but I read the papers too and I fail to see why the two should be mutually exclusive.

Gary is what I would call 'a solipsistic ironist'; he

seems to play up to the footballer image of being not very bright and pretends not to know things. Then he takes the piss out of you for assuming he was so thick.

Rory McGrath used to delight and piss me off in equal measure. He's a likeable guy, a man's man, but his neverending jokes about sportswomen having moustaches used to drive me nuts and I tried to counteract him at every possible point in the proceedings.

Jonathan Ross, who was a team captain for a while, was also very lovable but would occasionally dive into comedy rants about things I thought were unacceptable. He knew that these would never be transmitted as they were too near to the knuckle, but sometimes his comments used to get on my nerves. Oh yes, yes, I can hear some of you say, political correctness gone mad. However to me, the existence of political correctness is a GOOD THING because it protects the vulnerable. It is only a handful of silly people who have taken it too far and have laid themselves open to well-deserved derision, taking with them the rest of the gang who are only trying to improve the lives of those who have historically been treated like shit. To me there is nothing worse than watching white, wealthy, middle-class privileged men having a pop at people who have less ability and confidence to protect themselves.

*QI* is always a joyful experience. I love doing it. Alan Davies is a friend, so I get a chance to see him, but it's good fun working with Stephen Fry too. Being in the presence of his gargantuan brain makes me feel about five years old. *QI* has a gloriously loyal following and usually the audience know more than the panel does. The recording takes a good two hours and how they fit it into half an hour, I do not know. I think the feel-good factor on *QI* is down to the producer John Lloyd, who is a talented, highly intelligent and lovable man who has a great sense of humour and has been behind many of TV's comedy successes like *Not the Nine O'Clock News* and *Spitting Image*. You may think he has given me some money to eulogise him, but he hasn't.

## Never Mind the Buzzcocks

This was a show I always loved doing because it was hosted by my friend Mark Lamarr and therefore, saddo that I am, it gave me an opportunity to socialise. Like *They Think It's All Over* was a mixture of comics and sports-people, so *Buzzcocks* was a mix of musicians and comics. I am hardly the world's expert on music, so I never really knew the answers to questions, but I suppose that didn't matter and that's not why people were watching anyway. They wanted laughs.

It was quite a blokey show and the few women performers from the music industry tended to be there to be decorative rather than anything else. I remember though being on the show with Sporty Spice as she was then known, and bloody hell, could that woman talk; none of us could get a word in edgeways.

Sometimes I would have a great time on it and things would go brilliantly, because as a comic you cannot help being aware of the laughs-count in your head. Other times, I would slink away from it feeling that I'd done really badly and they wouldn't book me again because I was so rubbish. In those situations I just had to wait for a couple of days to pass and then I would forget about it and move on.

# Steam Radio

I love the radio, always have done. First of all, you don't have to sit down and look at it and secondly you can multi-task while you're listening, which is what all us women love to do.

I have worked mainly on Radios 2 and 4, and also on what was once known as GLR and is now called BBC London.

My first foray into radio started fairly early on in my comedy career when I was invited to do bits and pieces of comedy and stand-up on a show called *Hey RRradio!* which was presented by John Hegley and Patrick Marber. I have always been a huge admirer of John Hegley, whom I have mentioned elsewhere in this book. He is a comedy genius and I do not know why he isn't really famous. He has a cult following of people who absolutely adore him. This may actually be a more comfortable place to sit on the entertainment scale, as once you get a telly profile, lots of problems come with that. (This sounds as if I don't like Patrick, which is not true!)

*Hey RRadio!* was recorded in the charming rural hamlet of Woolwich in South-East London at The Tramshed, which was an old tramshed, handily enough. It was probably nearest to a comedy gig as anything could be without being a comedy gig and therefore was very comfortable to do. Basically we did the show to the audience while someone turned a tape recorder on, taped it and then snipped out the crap bits and then it went on the radio.

As time moved on, my comedy profile improved with the more telly that I did. Way back in the nineties there was a show on the radio called *The Mary Whitehouse Experience* which was an early version of the TV show of the same name. The show consisted of me, David Baddiel, Rob Newman, Punt and Dennis (Hugh Dennis of *Outnumbered* and *Mock the Week* fame) and a singing duo called Skint Video who were big on the comedy circuit. The producer was one Armando Iannucci who I'm sure you know (*The Thick of It*).

The show was recorded in front of a studio audience in one of the radio theatres and had songs, stand-up and sketches in it.

One day, as I arrived for rehearsal in the afternoon, I was handed a sketch to do. Being the only woman, I tended to get all the 'lady' roles. The sketch (short and sweet) consisted of me coming on stage to very loud American-style whooping and cheering and saying, 'Oh dear, I've forgotten to put my pants on.'

Well, I don't know if I was feeling particularly arsey that day, but I protested about why it had to be me who did that line, arguing that it would be funnier if a man said it. However, this was not accepted and I was told it was a line for a woman to do. So, rather grumpily I agreed to do it, but it niggled at me and when the time came round for me to perform it in front of the audience, I decided to take the line in my own way through to its logical conclusion.

So I stepped on stage to the sound of whooping and cheering and said, 'Oh fuck it, I think my quim's showing.'

Well, it got a really big laugh with a few gasps thrown in.

Unfortunately/fortunately it wasn't live. Had it been, I would probably never have worked on radio again.

Other favourite forays in the early years included:

## *Windbags*

*Windbags* was a show which I presented with stand-up Donna McPhail. Donna was a very sharp and dry stand-up who had worked on the circuit for years, and her fast speech and habit of jumping from topic to topic was a real contrast to my rather slow and laconic delivery. We used a tune for the top of the show by Rhoda & The Special AKA called 'Old Boiler' which is actually a rather scary and unsavoury song about a woman who gets raped. Yes, cheery, I know. We only had the instrumental lead-up in the show, so unless you were an aficionado of Two Tone, you wouldn't even have noticed.

We only interviewed women on the show, and our guests included Barbara Windsor, Caroline Aherne and Candida Doyle, keyboard player for the band Pulp. I asked her a question about Jarvis Cocker with whom I had appeared in bed on the front of the *New Musical Express*. (Well, be honest, that was the only way I was ever going to get into bed with *him*.) Candida refused to answer the question, saying, 'He wouldn't talk about me in an interview so why should I talk about him?' Quite right too.

The show ran for a couple of series but sadly never got recommissioned for a third despite having very high listener satisfaction ratings (whatever that means).

## GLR/Radio London

I loved my time at GLR/Radio London. Although it was a local radio station, because it was London it felt quite cosmopolitan and we were able to get great guests on. Initially I had a music show on which I was allowed to play what I liked – what a joy to be able to impose one's musical taste on everyone else. Although I am obviously a bit of an adolescent as I tended to pick songs (completely unconsciously) which had swear words in them. On one morning I remember I had picked 'Little Boy Soldiers' by The Jam and 'Working-Class Hero' by John Lennon. Halfway through 'Little Boy Soldiers' I saw a strange expression cross the face of the techie on the show. He realised a 'fuck' was coming up and leaped towards some dials and just managed to dip the sound before the offending word blasted round London. He wasn't so lucky with the Lennon song, but we apologised and I don't think there were that many complaints anyway.

Perhaps my favourite show on BBC London which GLR then became, was an interview show on Sunday mornings where I would be given a pretty heavyweight guest to interview from the world of politics or the arts. Among my best guests were Mo Mowlam, Vanessa Redgrave and Michael Foot.

Mo Mowlam was as full of life and humour as you would imagine. Very bright, sparky and relaxed. Speaking to her was enormously enjoyable and fun. By contrast, Vanessa Redgrave was scary as anything. Erudite, confident and as true a member of the arts aristocracy as you could get. I felt as if I was interviewing a headmistress, and was desperate not to put a foot wrong. Thankfully I didn't and we got on well, but I did feel like a naughty schoolgirl who hadn't done her homework.

Michael Foot had been my hero for a very long time and we had corresponded on a number of occasions. Our birthdays are on the same day and we exchanged cards for a bit and little presents. He was an intellectual giant with whom I could not possibly keep up. His career came to an abrupt halt when he was spotted at the Cenotaph one Remembrance Sunday wearing a donkey jacket, God forbid, and the press slaughtered him for not being smart enough in front of Her Maj. Oh, for God's sake, even if he had been wearing a donkey jacket, so what? It is the coat of the good honest working classes. Anyway, it wasn't a donkey jacket, it just looked like one and was remarked upon in a positive way by the Queen Mum. So there. (Obviously the fact that the Queen Mum's taste in clothes made her look like a drag queen will go unremarked here.)

By the time I interviewed Michael Foot he was in his late eighties and it wasn't easy. His hearing wasn't great and he became fixated on one particular area of Labour policy. He was impossible to interrupt because he couldn't hear me, so the whole thing was a bit of a nightmare. But I didn't care. He was Michael Foot and he was wonderful. Everyone said he was too gentle and nice to be in politics. Well, what an indictment of politics.

**Radio Cover**

For a few years, I covered on Radio 2 with Mark Lamarr for Jonathan Ross's holidays on Saturday mornings. This meant Christmas, Easter and five to six weeks in the summer. It was really great fun. Mark, as I've said, is a good friend so it was a real pleasure to work with him. Bands would play live in his studio and we had a stream of interesting, talented and occasionally slightly bonkers guests.

Mark has an encyclopaedic knowledge of music and would sort out the playlist, which he would bring in from his own collection, and every week I would bring along some CDs and try to sneak them in, which was not easy, particularly if they were performers he didn't like. Morrissey wasn't his favourite and he would make his disapproval clear by disappearing to the lav whenever I tried to force Morrissey on. Ditto Take That and Kate Bush and many others.

One of my favourite guests was Martha Reeves (her of Martha and the Vandellas) who really is a pop legend. She seemed constantly bemused by me and Mark, but joined in with enthusiasm. I am not sure how old she is, but at her age I would have been in bed with a hot-water bottle and a bowl of Complan, not slogging it round the world on planes.

It's such a weird situation when you get to meet some of your heroes and heroines. Nick Lowe was pure joy in every way, as was Jimmy Perry who wrote *Dad's Army*. I was sad when the job came to an end, but as I said earlier, when the top dogs change jobs, brooms start to sweep clean, and it's entirely possible you might be swept out on your arse.

# Writing This Effing Book

Writing this book has been bloody hard work. Not in the sense of working in the fields or down a mine, but just the sheer volume of words required to make up a whole book is terrifying when you stare at a blank computer screen and try to think of a witty first sentence.

I have a degree in work avoidance and will do almost anything to sidestep getting down to work. My strategies include tidying up. The only time I ever tidy up is when I'm shying away from getting down to work, and as I do this with remarkable frequency, my house is extremely tidy. Another favourite 'displacement activity' is Finding a Pointless Task That Doesn't Really

Need Doing. This could be something like getting out a map to look up the route to a gig I'm doing in two months' time, even though I have a satnav, or phoning up one of my friends who I know will be on the phone for ages. Or any of the following:

Trying to find my passport for a holiday next year

Cleaning my laptop

Reorganising my drawers – the wooden things with clothes in, not my pants

Checking my emails

Checking whether the post has come

Going to the shops to buy something I don't need, like stain-remover

Playing *Bubble Boom Challenge*

Handwashing a pile of 'Handwash Only' clothes that have been in a pile under my bed for three years

Crushing up cans for recycling so they are marginally smaller

Sorting out piles of stuff in my office into other piles

Doing the crossword in the paper

. . . and so on ad infinitum.

# Which Celebrities
# Are Arseholes?

This is a difficult question to answer, since on the whole, most famous people I meet tend to be pretty polite – possibly because they may consider me to be a celebrity too. So you have to examine how they treat those they may consider to be 'lesser mortals', like runners (the lowest stratum in TV, the poor sods who have to make the tea or go to the shop and try to find a chocolate éclair with fish oil in it), and it's not very often you get to see these interactions.

In my experience, the well-known stars in our culture who are accorded the title 'National Treasure' do tend to be National Nightmares, with a few notable exceptions like Julie Walters. Conversely, lots of people the tabloids try to encourage us to hate are perfectly sweet and decent people.

I once took my nephews, who were thirteen and fifteen at the time and moved their lips roughly once a month, to see *TFI Friday* and watch the proceedings. I loved that show, because it was at the Riverside Studios in Hammersmith, which is one of my favourite places. It backs onto the river, according it fantastic views of the sort of goings-on that go on near water – like boats, joggers along the towpath, swimmers occasionally, and birds.

The show was a hotchpotch of music, interviews and general silliness presented by Chris Evans, and my favourite character on it was The Lord of Love, played by the veteran actor Ronald Fraser, star of many sixties' films who had one of those instantly recognisable faces, but not a name that went with it. As The Lord of Love he would sit in a comfy chair and recite love poems to women in the audience. When I met him he said to me, 'If I was twenty years younger, I'd chase you all round Europe.' As a woman who tends not to garner compliments from men, I was hugely entertained by this and retain a fondness for his daftness to this day.

After the show I introduced Chris Evans to my nephews and expected him to give them a cursory hello and then bugger off to more interesting people. However, to his credit, he sat and talked to them for a good half an hour and even though they were too dumbstruck to reply a lot of the time, he kept at it and I know it really meant a lot to them, and certainly did to me.

Apologies if I have not peppered this section with scandal-laden slag-offs of celebs. If that's what you're after, buy the *Daily Mail*.

# The End

Hello, and congratulations. Welcome to the end of this book. Please feel free to prop a door open with it (which you may already have done) or draw a moustache on the picture of me on the front. God knows, women of my age struggle with that, as Trinny and Susannah have made perfectly clear to me in the past. The only thing I hope is that you've got something out of it – a few laughs, an idea for a new book to read, an insight into the comedy scene in the eighties and nineties, or perhaps some new ways to avoid getting down to something you don't want to get down to.

And rest assured, this comes up to the present day in my life, so I won't be picking up my trusty electronic pen for a good few years to come, God willing. Now go and have a multi-ingredient sandwich.

The (real) End

# JO BRAND

# Sorting Out Billy

Sarah is besotted with Billy, her unpredictable boyfriend. But after another outburst of his bad temper, Sarah's friends Martha and Flower decide that enough is enough. What should they do? Reason with him? Send him to anger management classes? Hire a hit man?

Martha and Flower have issues too. Martha is pregnant by three possible blokes, and hippy Flower's career as a stand-up comic is more sit-down-and-weep after a tongue-lashing by London's finest hecklers.

Can Martha survive single motherhood on a council estate in need of a peace-keeping force? Will Flower find the perfect put-down? And will they sort out Billy before he gets to them first?

Praise for Jo Brand's novels:

'A laugh-a-page tale . . . highly readable and genuinely funny' Alan Davies

'A smart stylist with a confident narrative voice. An accomplished comedy of romantic bad manners' *Observer*

'There isn't one dull passage. You could open the book at random, throw a dart and find something droll, well-observed and hard to forget' *Sunday Express*

978 0 7553 2030 1

headline
review

## JO BRAND

# It's Different for Girls

Rachel and Susan do *not* like to be beside the seaside. Hastings is so *uncool*.

Plunging headfirst into the choppy waters of adolescence, they are determined to survive their teens by sticking together. It's a rollercoaster ride of nutty parents, randy language students, stoned hippies, all-night parties on the pier, and an amusement arcade of emotional neediness.

But then Dave, sophisticated art student and unobtainable older boyfriend, enters their lives and everything changes between them. But when the girls find themselves together in London, they discover that their dreams of sex, drugs and rock 'n' roll don't quite match the reality . . .

Praise for Jo Brand's novels:

'A wonderfully funny and inventive novel' Stephen Fry

'A smart stylist with a confident narrative voice. An accomplished comedy of romantic bad manners' *Observer*

'There isn't one dull passage. You could open the book at random, throw a dart and find something droll, well-observed and hard to forget' *Sunday Express*

978 0 7553 2230 5

headline
**review**

Now you can buy any of these bestselling
books by **Jo Brand** from your bookshop
or *direct from her publisher*.

FREE P&P AND UK DELIVERY
(Overseas and Ireland £3.50 per book)

| | |
|---|---|
| The More You Ignore Me | £6.99 |
| It's Different For Girls | £7.99 |
| Sorting Out Billy | £7.99 |
| Look Back In Hunger | £7.99 |

TO ORDER SIMPLY CALL THIS NUMBER

**01235 400 414**

or visit our website: www.headline.co.uk

Prices and availability subject to change without notice.